RAND NATIONAL DEFENSE RESEARCH INSTITUTE

An Evaluation of the Department of Defense's Excess Property Program

Law Enforcement Agency Equipment Acquisition Policies, Findings, and Options

Aaron C. Davenport, Jonathan William Welburn, Andrew Lauland, Annelise Pietenpol, Marc Robbins, Erin Rebhan, Patricia Boren, K. Jack Riley

Prepared for the Defense Logistics Agency

For more information on this publication, visit www.rand.org/t/RR2464

Library of Congress Cataloging-in-Publication Data is available for this publication.
ISBN: 978-1-9774-0071-0

Published by the RAND Corporation, Santa Monica, Calif.

Cover image by Florence County North Carolina Sheriff's Department.

Preface

Section 1048 of the 2017 National Defense Authorization Act (NDAA) requires an evaluation of the Law Enforcement Support Office (LESO) program, which is run by the Defense Logistics Agency (DLA) and provides excess Department of Defense (DoD) equipment—everything from printers to rifles to airplanes—to state and federal law enforcement agencies (LEAs). The NDAA requires DoD to select a federally funded research and development center to review the program. RAND's National Defense Research Institute (NDRI) was asked to undertake that review, documented in this report. This evaluation builds upon previous work RAND researchers completed for DoD in 2016, in accordance with the fiscal year (FY) 2017 NDAA mandate for additional analysis of the LESO program.

This research was sponsored by the Defense Logistics Agency and conducted within the Acquisition and Technology Policy Center of the RAND National Defense Research Institute, a federally funded research and development center sponsored by the Office of the Secretary of Defense, the Joint Staff, the Unified Combatant Commands, the Navy, the Marine Corps, the defense agencies, and the defense Intelligence Community.

For more information on the Acquisition and Technology Policy Center, see www.rand.org/nsrd/ndri/centers/atp or contact the director (contact information is provided on the webpage).

Contents

Figures

Tables and Lists

Tables

Lists

Summary

The Law Enforcement Support Office Program

Since 1990, DoD has transferred $6 billion in excess property to LEAs in the United States.[1] Under the "1033 Program,"[2] as it is sometimes called, the LESO branch of the DLA can give LEAs excess DoD property at little or no cost.

At first glance, the program is straightforward: When military services and other DoD components no longer need a piece of equipment—anything from a desk to a truck to a rifle or other firearm—they turn it over to DLA for reuse, transfer, donation, sale, or destruction. After DLA offers the equipment to other DoD entities, qualified LEAs can requisition the equipment to assist in their law enforcement mission—border, counterdrug, and counterterrorism missions are given preference. If an LEA does not requisition the equipment, it is offered to other federal agencies outside law enforcement before being donated to states, sold to the public, or destroyed. To date, approximately 8,000 LEAs have obtained equipment through this program.

Although the list of equipment is extensive, not all DoD equipment is available to LEAs; DLA destroys items such as weapon system components, specialized military aircraft, armaments, and other exclusively military equipment.[3] However, some excess

---

1 The Law Enforcement Support Office (LESO) facilitates a *law enforcement support program*, which originated from the National Defense Authorization Act (NDAA) of Fiscal Year (FY) 1997. U.S. Code, Title 10 Section 2576a, Excess Personal Property: Sale or Donation for Law Enforcement Activities, authorized the Secretary of Defense to transfer excess property to law enforcement agencies (LEAs). The Defense Logistics Agency (DLA) manages the *LESO program* on behalf of the Department of Defense (DoD).

2 The name comes from the section number (1033) of the 1997 National Defense Authorization Act that codified the program into 10 U.S.C. 2576a. It is also commonly referred to as the *LESO program*. We use that term throughout this report.

3 RAND researchers in context to the LESO program define *military equipment* as that which possesses military attribute(s), may require further demilitarization before transfer, and/or is assigned a special DoD code that indicates a uniquely military feature, which may predetermine its disposition within the excess property system. The official definition of *military equipment* is codified in U.S. Code, Title 10, Section 2228, Office of Corrosion Policy and Oversight: "The term 'military equipment' includes all weapons systems, weapon platforms, vehicles, and munitions of the Department of Defense, and the components of such items."

military equipment, such as armored vehicles, is available. These are categorized by the LESO program as *controlled*, as described in more detail next.

Much of the equipment transferred by LESO is not controversial. Items such as office furniture, trailers, emergency generators and lighting, computers, and first aid and personal protective equipment help augment law enforcement activities, generally without creating the impression of contributing to the militarization of the police. Program participants use the military excess property to augment their resources and help meet their special equipment requirements for less routine activities, such as mass casualty response, natural and manmade disaster assistance, and large security events or civil disobedience incidents. However, LESO has long recognized the potential for transfer of military equipment to be viewed differently. For more than a decade, therefore, LESO has designated transfers of certain military equipment—such as firearms, night vision goggles, and most wheeled and tracked vehicles—as *controlled*. Controlled equipment has been subjected to additional rules, including the need to make it available for periodic inspections and the requirement to return it to LESO when no longer needed by the LEA. Additionally, controlled equipment ownership is retained by DoD and never permanently transferred to LEAs.

The 2014 shooting death of Michael Brown by a Ferguson, Missouri, police officer and the subsequent police response to protests and riots led to scrutiny of LESO program transfers. Although no LESO program equipment was involved in the events at Ferguson, the presence of armored personnel carriers focused public attention on the use of military equipment by the police and the relationship between transferred equipment, communities, and law enforcement. Some pointed to police possession and use of military equipment as proof of the militarization of police and suggested that the LESO program was a contributing factor. Proponents of the program, however, argued that reuse of DoD equipment was good stewardship of taxpayer dollars and that it contributed to officer and community safety.

In response to the events of Ferguson and after extensive study, President Obama issued Executive Order (EO) 13688, "Federal Support of Local Law Enforcement Equipment Acquisition," which separated military equipment provided by the program into three categories: prohibited, controlled, and uncontrolled. Prohibited items include tracked armored vehicles, aircraft with weapons, grenade launchers, and camouflage uniforms. Controlled items include riot batons, unmanned aerial vehicles, wheeled armored vehicles, and fixed and rotary wing aircraft. Uncontrolled material—such as hand and power tools, desks and filing cabinets, and first aid equipment—makes up the third category. Under this EO, if an LEA wants to acquire controlled equipment, it must provide valid justification for needing it. It must provide evidence of having received training on the proper use of the equipment, as well as on civil rights and civil liberties. And it is required to seek approval from the civilian governing body in its community. The bulk of the items on the prohibited list were already prohibited before the EO; a few items (e.g., tracked vehicles, bayonets, and camouflage personal protective equipment) were added. In interviews, LESO staff, state coordinators, and LEA officials reported little change in operations or in the equipment that LEAs obtained from the program as a result of this EO.

In August 2017, President Trump revoked EO 13688 when he issued EO 13809 "Restoring State, Tribal, and Local Law Enforcement's Access to Life-Saving Equipment and Resources." LESO is reverting to operating procedures prior to EO 13688 and is committed to administering the program without interruption. Due to the provisions of EO 13809, all references to EO 13688 and subsequent changes to policy pursuant to EO 13688 must be rescinded. However, few significant changes are expected in the types or quantities of equipment that LEAs requisition.

RAND's Evaluation of the Program

Public perception, as well as the political back and forth, puts the LESO program in a state of continuous change, and Congress has indicated it will carefully evaluate the program's future again in 2018. This report, which was mandated in section 1048 of the 2017 NDAA, is part of that effort. Specifically, RAND was asked to provide an evaluation of the program. To do this, we reviewed relevant literature and compiled a history of the program. DLA provided raw data on the participating LEAs, the equipment they requisitioned (including item counts and dollar values), the LEAs that had been suspended or terminated from the program, and equipment transfers among LEAs. We also examined whether DoD declares equipment as "excess" and then rebuys the same equipment soon thereafter—we refer to this as "rebuys."

We interviewed DLA officials at LESO headquarters in Battle Creek, Michigan, and we attended LESO's annual training conference for state-appointed coordinators in Norfolk, Virginia, where we spoke with state coordinators from 20 states and two U.S. territories. We interviewed LEA points of contact at 23 participating agencies, including top users of the program; we talked with officials at LEAs that have been suspended from the program within the past three fiscal years and with staff at LEAs that have been accused of militarization or have had recent police traumas. We spoke with key stakeholders, including congressional staffers, investigators from the Government Accountability Office (GAO), representatives from the National Association for the Advancement of Colored People (NAACP), the International Association of Campus Law Enforcement Administrators, the Police Foundation, and the National Organization of Black Law Enforcement Executives.[4] Finally, we assessed citizen knowledge and perceptions of the program using a survey through RAND's American Life Panel,

[4] We contacted the American Civil Liberties Union (ACLU), but representatives did not give us an interview opportunity.

which is a nationally representative, probability-based panel of U.S. citizens over the age of 18. Combined, these approaches produced a broad evaluation of the program.

Findings

Amount and Value of Transfers

In fiscal years 2015 to 2017, over 2.2 million uncontrolled items worth nearly $1.2 billion,[5] and over 3,000 controlled items worth nearly $775 million, were transferred to 2,790 state and local LEAs (henceforth jointly referred to as state LEAs),[6] 174 federal LEAs, and 22 tribal LEAs. State LEAs received the vast majority of LESO equipment in both quantity and value. Of the 2,790 state LEAs, 1,332 received controlled items; of the 174 federal LEAs, 17 received controlled items; and of the 22 tribal LEAs, 13 received controlled items.

LEAs requisition more uncontrolled property than controlled property. However, the controlled property represents larger dollar values. The following bullet points provide a snapshot of the program in FY 2016:

- LEAs held nearly 1.6 million items valued at nearly $1.9 billion dollars.
- LEAs acquired over 670,000 controlled items, which accounted for 82 percent of the total dollar value of equipment (or over $1.5 billion).
- While no transfers of prohibited equipment were made following EO 13688, interviews and analysis of LESO data sets reveal that numerous (5,591) prohibited items, amounting to a total value of $418,772, remained in LEA possession. The vast majority of these items are camouflaged clothing, personal protective equipment, and nonlethal riot control tactical gear.
- Uncontrolled items obtained by LEAs numbered nearly 900,000, with a total value of over $339 million.
- For controlled property, 1 percent of all LEAs held 25 percent of the total quantity of property and 30 percent of the total value.
- For uncontrolled property, 1 percent of all LEAs held 50 percent of the total quantity and 30 percent of the total value.
- In total, 10 percent of LEAs received 73 percent of uncontrolled items.

Types of Items Transferred

From hand warmers to laptops to rifles, over 7,000 unique types of items were transferred to LEAs through the LESO program in FYs 2015 to 2017. Of the property held by LEAs, the top 20 items, in terms of dollar value, made up 80 percent of all property

---

5 Monetary values, which reflect the original DoD purchase price, are based on data from the Federal Excess Property Management Information System (FEPMIS).

6 State LEAs include territorial, tribal, state, sheriff, city, town, and municipal police departments that employ sworn officers with arrest authority and meet the requirements for participation in the LESO program.

transfers. When ranking the value of equipment transferred, 14 of the top 20 item types were vehicles, including trucks and fixed- and rotary-wing aircraft. Mine resistant ambush protected (MRAP) vehicles alone made up 31 percent of the total dollar value of property held by LEAs. In terms of quantity, magazine cartridges were the most frequent item transferred. Other items frequently transferred included rifles, field packs, reflex sights, tourniquets, flashlights, and first aid kits.

We found no clear relationship between LEA size and equipment acquisitions. However, about one-third of MRAP vehicles had been acquired by LEAs with fewer than 50 sworn officers and close to two-thirds by those with fewer than 100.[7]

Suspensions and Terminations

During FYs 2014 to 2016, there were 268 LEA suspensions and 24 LEA terminations from the program. Of the 268 total suspensions, 267 were of state, one was of tribal, and none was of federal LEAs. Of the 267 suspensions at the state level, 23 percent were in North Carolina, and 10 percent were in Montana. Eight states/territories—Alabama, Alaska, North Carolina, New Jersey, Minnesota, Ohio, Rhode Island, and the U.S. Virgin Islands—were suspended in their entirety. The most frequent justification for LEA suspensions were lost, missing, or stolen weapons; followed by state coordinator requests for termination, citing chronic lack of LEA compliance with program requirements as the major driver; followed by protracted issues with resolution and final disposition of lost, missing, or stolen weapons.

Department of Defense "Rebuys"

As noted in the FY 2017 NDAA language, there is specific congressional concern about the LESO program and whether DoD is declaring property excess and then purchasing the same item soon after. In April 2016, Senator Claire McCaskill submitted follow-up questions to DoD, pursuant to the Senate Homeland Security and Governmental Affairs Committee hearing, "Oversight of Federal Programs for Equipping State and Local Law Enforcement," held in September 2014. Senator McCaskill expressed concern that DoD was declaring as excess a number of items that were in new or like-new condition and giving them away to state and local law enforcement and other federal agencies while purchasing new versions of those same items in the same year.[8] Senator McCaskill's question applies broadly to more transfers than those in the LESO program. DoD provides excess property through at least ten special programs. To provide a more complete and conclusive answer, an in-depth analysis of all

---

7 Based upon a 2015 Department of Justice, Bureau of Justice Statistics report, about half of the more than 12,000 police departments in the United States employed fewer than 10 officers (Brian A. Reaves, *Local Police Departments 2013: Personnel, Policies, and Practices*, NCJ 248677, Washington, D.C.. U.S. Department of Justice, Office of Justice Programs, Bureau of Justice Statistics, May 2015).

8 Principal Deputy Under Secretary of Defense, Acquisition, Technology, and Logistics, "Oversight of Federal Programs for Equipping State and Local Law Enforcement," letter to U.S. Senator Claire McCaskill, January 19, 2017.

DoD component purchasing data and all excess property transfers made, regardless of the recipient and the specialty program, is recommended. This focus is beyond the scope of the evaluation DLA asked RAND to complete and would take significantly more time, special data handling, and access to DoD component purchasing data. Without access to all of DoD's purchasing data across all DoD components over the five-year period, a full analysis is not possible.[9]

Program Perceptions

Congress

Interest in the LESO program remains high as congressional members field inquiries from constituents. These inquiries generally fall into three categories. The first relates to good stewardship of government funds and property; the second, to inappropriately equipping LEAs with military equipment; and the third, to parity with other government programs that provide equipment to state and local agencies. Congress is particularly interested in the issue of parity.

Regarding parity, state and local fire departments, public works departments, prison and highway systems, and emergency response agencies not affiliated with law enforcement would also like the opportunity to screen and requisition DoD excess property. The majority of excess property offered through the LESO program is not specifically unique to law enforcement activities or policing. Some LESO critics argue that hand and power tools, emergency generators, earth-moving and excavating equipment, all-terrain vehicles, and emergency medical supplies could benefit many more organizations than just LEAs. Currently, government agencies without sworn officers with arrest authority must wait until later in the excess property process to requisition equipment and are in competition with other programs. In a GAO report released in January 2016,[10] investigators made a point of illustrating various types and quantities of equipment being transferred to LEAs that would not necessarily be perceived as directly applicable to law enforcement activities (e.g., forklifts, cranes, tractors, dump trucks, musical instruments, and food service equipment).

Government Accountability Office (GAO)

The LESO program has been the subject of ongoing GAO attention since its inception. Over the years, GAO has issued eight reports identifying issues with DoD's overall management of excess property and made 24 separate recommendations for enhancing internal controls and improving program efficiency related to the LESO program.

---

[9] Discussions with DLA and LESO staff in August 2017 indicated that access to multiple purchasing databases and analysis of very large data sets is beyond the scope of this evaluation and would require considerably more time, special coordination, and cooperation from multiple customers to provide conclusive results. The DoD response provides an estimation or approximation of rebuy, based on readily available DLA data.

[10] GAO, *Excess Personal Property: DOD Should Further Reassess the Priorities of Its Disposal Process*, GAO-16-44, January 29, 2016.

DLA has implemented 22 of these recommendations that were within its scope. The recommendations that have yet to be implemented relate to DoD-wide excess property policy, which is still pending resolution and is beyond DLA's authority. Resolution has been stalled further due to the revocation of EO 13688 and efforts to implement the changes directed in EO 13809.[11]

GAO officials have expressed support for the program, though monitoring is likely to continue until there are no longer concerns about program accountability and oversight. Several issues are still relevant, including disposal of controlled equipment, verification of program requirements, and potential conflicts of interest associated with the appointment of state coordinators who both approve enrollments and requisitions and represent LEAs seeking equipment. There are instances of state coordinators who also serve as LEA points of contact.

State Program Coordinators

Based on our interviews, state program coordinators and LEAs regard the LESO program as valuable. State coordinators generally believe that categorizations of prohibited, controlled, and uncontrolled equipment are appropriate. When they do not, they most often indicate that categorizations are too restrictive. Many state coordinators say the most significant change in the program as a result of EO 13688 is the increased paperwork and justification required to acquire certain types of equipment.

Use of controlled equipment, according to most state coordinators, reduces risk to officers and citizens; they often cite the protective function of MRAPs during rescue operations, the use of robots for bomb threats or active-shooter response, and thermal imaging equipment to detect hidden subjects and victims. Several note that controlled LESO equipment is often available commercially and that the LESO program does not inherently increase risk to citizens. They indicate that the program does, however, allow LEAs to acquire equipment they might otherwise not be able to afford. State coordinators indicate that they take steps to ensure equipment requested through the LESO program is used for law enforcement purposes by carefully reviewing written justifications and conducting interviews of LEA operators when performing annual onsite program compliance reviews.

State coordinators also report that the LESO program relieves LEAs' budget constraints, increases officer safety, and improves preparedness. In making determinations about the appropriateness of equipment for LEAs, most state coordinators tell us that they rely on the justifications provided by LEAs in the requisition paperwork. Most do not believe that independent assessments are necessary. State coordinators do, however, point to public perceptions of the program or of law enforcement in general as cause for considering whether a piece of controlled equipment should be requisitioned. State

---

[11] DLA subject-matter expert (SME) interviews, August and September 2017.

coordinators tell us that they have not received any valid complaints about LEA use of LESO equipment, though they do field media inquiries.

LEA Staff

Respondents from LEAs generally endorse the program. Many say the categorizations of equipment are appropriate. A small number are critical of the way items are categorized. Most indicate that EO 13688 has not changed the types of equipment they requisition.

Many respondents indicate that the LESO program has saved their agencies hundreds of thousands to millions of dollars. Respondents from larger agencies tell us that they do not note a critical impact on equipment inventory—large agencies have been able to procure the same types of equipment through other channels. However, respondents from smaller agencies indicate they would not have been able to obtain either the controlled or uncontrolled items they acquired were it not for the LESO program.

Respondents note using LESO equipment for hostage and other high-threat situations, for periods of heightened security, and for humanitarian assistance and disaster response. Some say they have used medical equipment acquired from LESO to save lives. Others report that they no longer acquire controlled equipment due to public perceptions, while still others note they focus on education by working with the media, elected officials, and the community to improve understanding of the program. However, most LEAs report that their positions regarding whether to obtain and how to use certain types of equipment have not changed due to public perceptions, because they have always been careful when requisitioning equipment. Most respondents do not see any downsides to participating in the program.

Other Stakeholders

Other stakeholders (i.e., representatives from the NAACP, Police Foundation, Campus LEA Administrators, and National Organization of Black Law Enforcement Executives) acknowledge the value of the program to LEAs but remain concerned about the perceptions of inappropriately equipping police and about overall program integrity. Several reported being interested in the issue of police militarization even before the controversy surrounding the LESO program arose. Others indicated some equipment is not appropriate for LEAs to acquire, such as bayonets and assault rifles. These stakeholders advocate greater community awareness and responsible use of the equipment. Our research did not reveal any organization that advocates a complete abolition of transferring excess property to LEAs.

Stakeholders suggest that LEAs should receive training on equipment and that justifications for obtaining the equipment should be in line with the training. Some stakeholders express that transfers to LEAs should be limited or eliminated for controversial items, while others reported that additional oversight of the program is needed. The Police Foundation, for example, suggests that law enforcement experts should provide the guidance on equipment use. However, the Department of Justice (DOJ) currently defers to DoD on judging the appropriateness of justifications, since the transfer of equipment is managed by DLA. Despite concerns about perceptions, stakeholders acknowledge that the LESO program is an important resource for LEAs and can help in the performance of law enforcement missions.

Public Perceptions

To gain insight into public perceptions, we conducted a survey of 1,044 U.S. citizens through RAND's American Life Panel (ALP). The survey highlighted that many Americans are unaware of the program, indicating that additional public education and community outreach may increase public awareness; however, the idea of the program has the support of the majority, albeit with some restrictions. The bullets below summarize our key findings:

- Almost half of respondents (48 percent) report being unaware of programs that provide LEAs with excess military equipment, while 33 percent find military transfers valuable and 20 percent find them detrimental.
- 46 percent of participants support limiting the program (41 percent to nonlethal equipment and 5 percent to no equipment at all), while 38 percent do not think there should be any limitations, and the other 16 percent had no opinion.
- Program support is significantly lower among black and Hispanic participants, who are also less likely to know of the program than are white participants.

Future Options for the LESO Program

Overall, we find that the LESO program is being administered by DLA according to congressional intent. Program staff and officials are aware of their sensitive mission and the political and cultural issues surrounding it. DLA has responded diligently to reviews, and the evolution of the program reflects that. With each incarnation, stronger controls have been put in place.

Our analysis leaves one question unanswered, however: How can LESO, DLA, and, indeed, the U.S. government address the concern about the effect of LESO on the militarization of local police forces? Much of the criticism of the program from the media and sources outside of the federal government are centered around the appearance of the equipment that LEAs have in their possession or have employed. That is, despite a thorough and objective analysis pointing to a soundly managed program, the problem of police militarization—and LESO's role in that—is likely to remain for the foreseeable future. Within this context, we believe there are three potential paths forward.

Maintain the Status Quo

The first, perhaps obvious, option is to leave the program as is. As noted, we find that the LESO program is professionally managed. Although there are a few lagging issues regarding program administration and policy, satisfactory attention is paid to managing to congressional intent. The program is popular with LEAs, even if there are minor complaints about bureaucracy and program administration. DoD has a solid record of keeping track of controlled equipment. And the vast majority of transfers—measured in quantity—are of general office equipment, tools, personal protective equipment, and other noncontroversial material.

Modify Program Emphasis and Distribution of Controlled Equipment

The second option is to maintain the status quo with a few modifications. Currently, requisition priority is given to LEAs that provide specific justifications for border security, counternarcotics, and counterterrorism police activities. These preferential justifications for border, counterdrug, and counterterrorism missions are sensitive because the resultant law enforcement activities frequently put LEAs in direct contact with citizens.

One modification, therefore, would be to remove the preferential treatment given by the LESO program to drug, border, and terrorism missions. There are no conclusive assessments of whether this preferential treatment is distorting LESO requests and otherwise diluting public understanding of the real reasons why jurisdictions are requesting equipment.

Another modification could be to ensure that LESO is not the first provider of potentially controversial and high-visibility controlled equipment. Under such a scheme, an LEA requesting a high-mobility multipurpose wheeled vehicle (HMMWV), for example, would have to first procure—perhaps purchase—one from another source. This requirement would ensure that LEAs truly need a given item, would have previously justified the acquisition internally through their own budget process, and obtained permissions from their civilian leadership. Under this approach, DoD would be merely augmenting programs and methods established under community control and operation. One potential unintended consequence of this option is the high cost that smaller, less resourced LEAs would have to bear for the initial purchase of equipment, which may result in a reduction of the overall number of participating LEAs.

Shift Responsibility for Controlled Equipment to Another Organization

The final option for the program is to move responsibility for decisions about approving distribution and oversight of controlled equipment from DLA to another organization with law enforcement oversight responsibility, most likely DoJ. Under this approach, DLA could maintain responsibility for its disposition time line but pass responsibility for adjudicating individual controlled equipment requests to DoJ. DoJ would, in turn, signal DLA about specific equipment requests within the time line.

We propose this option because DoJ is better positioned than DoD to evaluate the appropriateness and value of equipment to law enforcement. Likewise, DoJ is better-positioned through its existing evaluation programs and its relations with LEAs to provide assessments on the impact of this program on policing.

DLA has been careful to minimize its involvement in domestic law enforcement activities, but the program, as it stands, necessarily requires DLA to pass judgment on the soundness and suitability of local law enforcement plans. Institutionally, DLA is poorly equipped for this role and has neither the expertise nor the credibility to fill this role effectively. In contrast, relocating most of the program responsibility to DoJ could lead to the development of more insight into the effectiveness and consequences of equipment transfers. Potential advances unlikely to materialize under DLA management, but that could very well materialize under DoJ management, include the following:

- the development of standards for monitoring the use and employment of controlled equipment
- the ability to link equipment transfers to police outcomes (via measures such as officer safety, crime rates, or police use of force)
- the ability to link equipment transfers to police activities (such as training, use and employment of transferred equipment, and the extent to which transfers permit chronic underfunding of law enforcement functions).

Acknowledgments

The authors would like to acknowledge the outstanding cooperation and assistance provided by the Defense Logistics Agency, Law Enforcement Support Office, DLA J-349, the various interagency stakeholders, nongovernmental organizations, advocacy groups, and the many state and local representatives of law enforcement who provided valuable information that was necessary to complete this evaluation. None of this would have been possible without the support, insight, advice, and guidance of our RAND colleagues: Cynthia Cook, Christopher Mouton, James Anderson, Melissa Bradley, Elina Treyger, Amanda Kadlec, RADM(ret) Tom Atkin, John Godges, Karen Edwards, David Grant, and Mark Hvizda.

Abbreviations

ACLU	American Civil Liberties Union
ALP	RAND American Life Panel
AMPS	Account Management and Provisioning Service
ASD(LMR)	Assistant Secretary of Defense for Logistics and Materiel Readiness
BJA	Bureau of Justice Assistance
CBP	Customs and Border Protection
CMIS	Computerized Management Information System
DDS	Defense Logistics Agency Disposition Services
DEA	Drug Enforcement Administration
DHS	Department of Homeland Security
DLA	Defense Logistics Agency
DoD	U.S. Department of Defense
DODAAC	Department of Defense Activity Address Code
DoJ	Department of Justice
EO	executive order
FBI	Federal Bureau of Investigation
FEDLOG	Federal Logistics Data on Mobile Media
FEPMIS	Federal Excess Property Management Information System
FFRDC	federally funded research and development center
FOP	Fraternal Order of Police
FSC	federal supply class

FY	fiscal year
GAO	Government Accountability Office
GSA	Government Services Administration
HAP	humanitarian assistance program
HASCOI	House Armed Services Committee, Subcommittee on Oversight and Investigations
HSGAC	Homeland Security and Governmental Affairs Committee
HMMWV	high-mobility multipurpose wheeled vehicle
H.R.	U.S. House Resolution
IACLEA	International Association of Campus Law Enforcement Administrators
IHE	institutes of higher education
LEA	law enforcement agency
LEEDS	Law Enforcement Equipment Data System
LESO	Law Enforcement Support Office
MARS	Military Affiliate Radio System
MOA	memorandum of agreement
MRAP	mine resistant ambush protected
NAACP	National Association for the Advancement of Colored People
NDAA	National Defense Authorization Act
NIJ	National Institute of Justice
NOBLE	National Organization of Black Law Enforcement Executives
NSN	national stock number
NTOA	National Tactical Officers Association
PCR	program compliance review
POC	point of contact
PWG	permanent working group
ROTC	Reserve Officers' Training Corps
RTD	Reutilization, Transfer, Donation
SECDEF	Secretary of Defense

SWAT	Special Weapons and Tactics
USDA	U.S. Department of Agriculture

CHAPTER ONE

Introduction

Section 1048 of the 2017 National Defense Authorization Act (NDAA) requires a thorough review of the Law Enforcement Support Office (LESO) program, which is run by the Defense Logistics Agency (DLA) and provides excess Department of Defense (DoD) equipment—everything from printers to rifles to airplanes—to state, territorial, tribal, and federal law enforcement agencies (LEAs). The NDAA requires DoD to select a federally funded research and development center (FFRDC) to review the program. RAND's National Defense Research Institute was asked to undertake the review, which is documented in this report.

In this first chapter, we step through the history of the program, which is essential context for understanding why the program is often the subject of review and scrutiny. In the next chapter, we describe the processes used to transfer equipment from the military services to LEAs, providing information on logistics as well as on which entities are involved in each step.

In Chapter Three, we describe the types of equipment that have been transferred over the past few years, where that equipment goes, and how much it is worth. We also discuss suspensions and terminations from the program and provide results from a preliminary examination of rebuys—that is, the equipment that DoD deemed excess and repurchased shortly after.

In Chapter Four we summarize our interviews with state coordinators, officials from LEAs, and other stakeholders in the program. In Chapter Five, we present the results from a survey we conducted through RAND's American Life Panel (ALP). In Chapter Six, we provide closing thoughts on potential ways to move the program forward—especially in light of the perception issues the program has faced and will continue to face for the foreseeable future.

History of the LESO Program

The United States has a long history of constitutional and legislative mandates to separate military operations from domestic policing. However, as expectations about the scope of government have evolved, so, too, has the role of policing in America.[1] Demands for safety often conflict with expectations of governmental restraint. As the front line of the government, police officers are often viewed as the litmus test of government indifference or overreach. Their actions can directly affect the public's perceptions of personal freedom or abuse of government authority. In policing, perceptions matter.

The LESO program, which, as noted, transfers excess DoD equipment to LEAs, falls squarely in the center of this conversation—and at the core of these perceptions. Because of its role in the perceived militarization of police, the LESO program has been scrutinized both publicly and congressionally, and it continues to be the source of debate in various stakeholder communities, as well as in the legislative and executive branches of government. To shed light on the debate, we recount the history of the program in this chapter. Figure 1.1 provides an abbreviated time line of sentinel events over the life of the LESO program, from its inception.

The Beginnings of the LESO Program

To help in combating the alarming spike in the flow of illegal drugs from South America and the subsequent increase in drug-related violence and deaths, Congress authorized DoD, through the NDAA, to assume a more prominent role in assisting other federal agencies with detecting and monitoring illegal drug production and trafficking.[2] Known as the "War on Drugs," this period began in the 1970s and reached its peak in the 1980s. During that time, Congress took steps to provide LEAs with drug-fighting tools. Congress authorized DoD to provide material support to federal, state, local, and tribal LEAs through the sale or donation of excess property in 10 U.S.C., 2576a.[3]

The NDAAs for FYs 1990 and 1991 allowed DoD to transfer excess property for counterdrug activities to federal and state agencies. The act was set to terminate in 1992 but was extended to 1997 by the enactment of section 1044 of the NDAA for FY 1993.[4] In 1995, DLA assumed management responsibilities of transferring excess DoD equipment.[5]

The FY 1997 NDAA allowed DoD to transfer or donate excess personal property to state, local, and tribal LEAs. Preference was given to LEAs that would use the prop-

---

[1] David Alan Sklansky, "Police and Democracy," *Michigan Law Review*, Vol. 103, No. 7, June 2005, pp. 1699–1830.

[2] Daniel H. Else, "The '1033 Program,' Department of Defense Support to Law Enforcement," Congressional Research Service, August 28, 2014, p. 1.

[3] U.S. Code, Title 10, Section 2576a, Excess Personal Property: Sale or Donation for Law Enforcement Activities.

[4] Else, 2014.

[5] Defense Logistics Agency, "Defense Logistics Agency Instruction DLAI 4140.11," December 22, 2016.

Figure 1.1
LESO Time Line

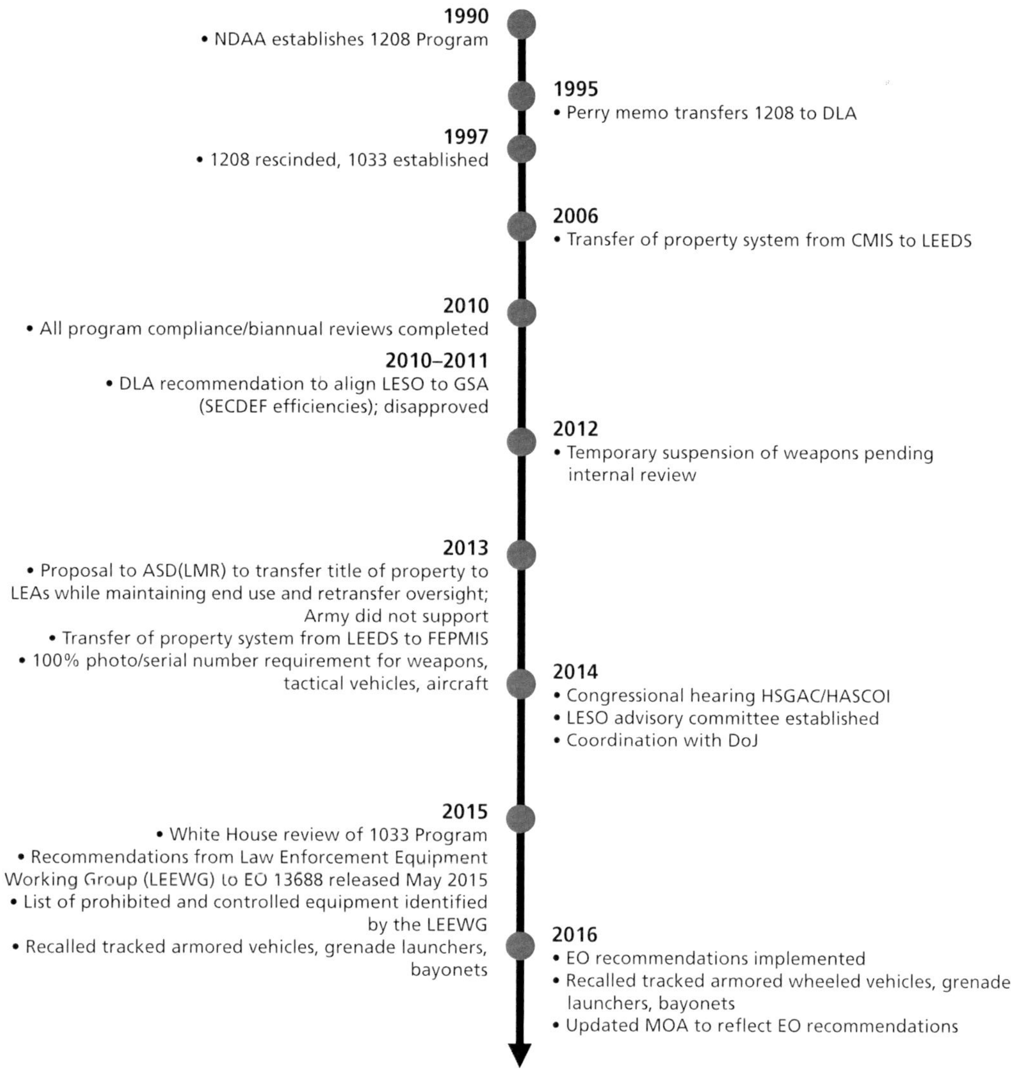

SOURCE: Carlos Torres, "Law Enforcement Support Office (LESO) Program," Federal Law Enforcement Agencies brief, Defense Logistics Agency Disposition Services, June 5, 2017.
NOTES: CMIS = Computerized Management Information System. LEEDS = Law Enforcement Equipment Data System. GSA = Government Services Administration. SECDEF= Secretary of Defense. ASD(LMR) = Assistant Secretary of Defense for Logistics and Materiel Readiness. FEPMIS = Federal Excess Property Management Information System. HSGAC = Homeland Security and Governmental Affairs Committee. HASCOI = House Armed Services Committee, Subcommittee on Oversight and Investigations. DoJ = Department of Justice. EO = executive order. MOA = memorandum of agreement.
RAND *RR2464-1.1*

erty for counterdrug or counterterrorism operations.[6] LEAs who took advantage of the program were required to pay for the costs of transferring the equipment, but DoD did not charge LEAs for assuming control of the property.

The program was regulated by the *Defense Materiel Disposition Manual*,[7] adopted in August 1997, which implemented procedures for the disposition of DoD's excess personal property. In 1999, policy guidance for the program moved from the DoD Coordinator for Drug Enforcement Policy and Support to the Assistant Deputy Under Secretary of Defense for Material and Distribution Management, though DLA still provided management and oversight,[8] as it has since 1995.

The Middle Years (2005–2013)

The LESO program operates as part of a larger DoD system, also operated by DLA, for collecting, reusing, and disposing of excess materiel. That larger system has attracted criticism and oversight in recent years.[9] The outcomes of the ensuing evaluations were not always favorable, and DLA has engaged in efforts to correct its deficits.

In 2005, the GAO released a report on waste and inefficiency in DoD, including LESO and several other excess property programs, titled *Management Control Breakdowns Result in Substantial Waste and Inefficiency*.[10] GAO found that DoD did not have controls in place to ensure excess property was reused effectively and efficiently. The report indicated that DoD would purchase new equipment when it had similar excess equipment that was in excellent condition. According to the report, root causes for the inefficiency included unreliable data, inadequate oversight, and outdated and nonintegrated inventory and supply management systems. GAO called for more data reliability, better physical inventory control, and more functional inventory systems. DoD implemented changes, but a follow-up investigation by GAO in 2006 indicated breakdowns in system controls and in security intended to keep sensitive equipment

6 How DoD verifies this is described in greater detail in later chapters. Use of key words and short explanations are provided on electronic requisition forms and approved by State Coordinators and DLA LESO program specialists.

7 U.S. Department of Defense Manual 4160.21-M, *Defense Materiel Disposition Manual*, Office of the Deputy Under Secretary of Defense (Logistics), Washington, D.C., August 1997.

8 Defense Logistics Agency, 2016.

9 See, for example, U.S. General Accounting Office (GAO), *Inventory Management: Better Controls Needed to Prevent Misuse of Excess DOD Property*, OSI/NSIAD-00-147, April 28, 2000; GAO, *Defense Inventory: Control Weaknesses Leave Restricted and Hazardous Excess Property Vulnerable to Improper Use, Loss, and Theft*, GAO-02-75, January 25, 2002; Office of the Inspector General, *Logistics: Law Enforcement Support Office Excess Property Program (D-2003-101)*, Washington, D.C., U.S. Department of Defense, June 13, 2003.

10 GAO, *DOD Excess Property: Management Control Breakdowns Result in Substantial Waste and Inefficiency*, GAO-05-277, Washington, D.C., June 7, 2005.

from being sold.[11] GAO also found that DoD continued to sell new and unused equipment for pennies on the dollar.

With respect to the LESO program, in May of 2012, DLA instituted a moratorium on weapons transfers after receiving reports of missing equipment and inappropriate weapons transfers during an annual inventory.[12] DLA maintained the moratorium until there were adequate controls in place to decrease the incidence of lost or stolen weapons. As a result of the moratorium, DLA changed policies and set the program on the path it is on today—one of compliance reviews and LEA suspensions for missing weapons. The moratorium on weapons transfers was lifted in 2013.[13]

Further process-related issues surfaced when the *Arizona Republic* reported on a controversy at the Pinal County, Arizona, sheriff's department, which had stockpiled over $7 million in LESO equipment with the intention of selling it at auction to boost its budget.[14] The sheriff also "loaned" equipment to other non-LEAs for one year and would then transfer title of the property to that agency. During the year, the non-LEA would pay for the insurance on the equipment. According to the article, several agencies were grateful for the support, recognizing that all of the agencies were working toward public safety. Other agency representatives felt the sheriff was using the equipment to build clout for his political career. The department was able to request this equipment because the state coordinator had appointed one of the Pinal County Sheriff's Department's employees as a point of contact for the LESO program.

An Era of Tumult (2014–Present)

Recent events have ignited and sustained a national debate about police militarization and the appropriateness of LEAs acquiring military equipment. We outline these events in a mostly chronological fashion, although the events overlapped in some cases.

American Civil Liberties Union and Government Accountability Office Reports

The American Civil Liberties Union (ACLU) released a report critical of the militarization of law enforcement in June of 2014.[15] The report argued that LEAs, specifically their Special Weapons and Tactics (SWAT) teams, were deploying heavily armed officers using dangerous tactics in situations that did not call for such heavy-handed responses. The report indicated that the number of SWAT deployments had increased

---

[11] GAO, *Control Breakdowns Present Significant Security Risk and Continuing Waste and Inefficiency*, GAO-06-943, Washington, D.C., July 25, 2006.

[12] Radley Balko, "Pentagon Suspends Program That Gives Military Weapons to Cops," *Huffington Post*, June 11, 2012.

[13] Based on interviews with DLA headquarters and DLA Disposition Services representatives, August–September 2017.

[14] Dennis Wagner, "Pinal Sheriff's Office Stockpiles, Prepares to Sell Military Equipment," *Arizona Republic*, May 19, 2012.

[15] ACLU, *War Comes Home: The Excessive Militarization of American Policing*, June 2014a.

in recent decades and that SWAT teams were called out for more reasons than they had been in the past.

The ACLU report argued that police escalated violence in police-community interactions and that minority community members were disproportionately targeted. The ACLU pointed to training officers in a "warrior" mentality as other evidence of police militarization. The ACLU report characterized materiel that had been provided to LEAs by the LESO program—specifically, mine resistant ambush protected (MRAP) vehicles and military-looking uniforms—as contributors to the militarization of police and more aggressive policing behavior. The ACLU recommended curbing the program.

Around the same time that the ACLU report was published in 2014, GAO released a report titled *Actions Needed to Improve the Defense Logistics Agency's Inventory Management*,[16] which focused on inventory management across DLA. GAO found that DLA had disposed of a significant amount of materiel that it might need to repurchase in the future. The report concluded that DLA's inventory management had weaknesses and could be bolstered using stronger methods for determining what is excess and what should be left in storage.

These reports set the stage for congressional scrutiny, in terms of both the effectiveness of the process and the appropriateness of providing police departments with excess military equipment. However, the events of August 2014 brought that scrutiny to the forefront of congressional and public concern.

Michael Brown and Ferguson, Missouri

On August 9, 2014, Michael Brown was shot and killed by a Ferguson, Missouri, police officer. Tensions between community members and the police boiled over, and protests and riots ensued. The police responded with what some saw as an overly heavy-handed approach.[17] Pictures circulated through the media of police officers wearing camouflage and sitting on top of armored vehicles with sniper rifles pointing toward crowds of citizens.[18] Although the equipment used by the police in this incident was not provided through the LESO program, the police appeared to many as a military entity rather than a civilian law enforcement agency. Naturally, all government programs providing equipment to LEAs were immediately scrutinized for cause and effect. In the media, the conversation about militarized police became more heated. LEAs across

[16] GAO, *Actions Needed to Improve the Defense Logistics Agency's Inventory Management*, GAO-14-495, Washington, D.C., June 19, 2014.

[17] Shirley Li, "The Evolution of Police Militarization in Ferguson and Beyond," *The Atlantic*, August 15, 2014; Paul D. Shinkman, "Ferguson and the Militarization of Police," *U.S. News*, August 14, 2014; Paul Szoldra, "This Is the Terrifying Result of the Militarization of Police," *Business Insider*, August 12, 2014.

[18] The reader can Google "Ferguson Protests and Police Militarization" to see the scope of the conversation and wide dissemination of photographs.

the country, including on college campuses, were scrutinized for their acquisition of military equipment.[19] Officials in Washington, D.C., responded.

President Obama expressed concern about the perceived militarization of the police, stating, "There is a big difference between our military and our local law enforcement and we don't want those lines blurred."[20] Less than three weeks after Michael Brown's death, the White House confirmed that President Obama had ordered a government-wide federal review of processes that provide military equipment to LEAs.[21] Congress prepared for its own review of the LESO program, and the Congressional Research Service released an overview of the program on August 28.[22]

On September 9, 2014, the Senate Committee on Homeland Security and Governmental Affairs held a hearing titled "Oversight of Federal Programs for Equipping State and Local Law Enforcement." Senators Thomas R. Carper, Tom Coburn, and Claire McCaskill heard witnesses on the structure and role of programs, notably the LESO program, that provide military equipment to LEAs, as well as perspectives favoring and opposing the program.[23]

Proponents of the LESO program, including representatives from the Police Foundation and National Tactical Officers Association (NTOA), argued that the equipment protects officers, supports counterdrug and counterterrorism operations, assists in disaster relief efforts, and relieves budgetary constraints. However, the appropriateness of the use of this type of equipment depends on the context and quality of police training.

Critics of the program—including a professor who studies police militarization, a St. Louis photojournalist, and a representative from the National Association for the Advancement of Colored People (NAACP)—argued that such programs allow LEAs to become overly militarized and dangerous, that heavily armed police officers escalate tensions with citizens, and that people of color are disproportionately negatively affected by this militarization. These opponents called for ending the rhetoric declaring war on the American people (i.e., the "War on Drugs" and the "War on Crime").

---

[19] Dan Bauman, "On Campus, Grenade Launchers, M-16s, and Armored Vehicles," *Chronicle of Higher Education,* September 11, 2014.

[20] Zeke J. Miller, "Obama Voices Concerns on Police Militarization in Wake of Ferguson," *Time,* August 18, 2014.

[21] ACLU, "Coalition Including ACLU Asks Defense Secretary for Moratorium on 1033 Program that Militarizes Local Police," press release, October 27, 2014b; White House Office of the Press Secretary, "Press Briefing by Press Secretary Josh Earnest, 8/25/2014," Washington, D.C., August 25, 2014.

[22] Else, 2014.

[23] "Are Federal Programs that Provide Military Equipment to State and Local Police Departments Effective?" *Congressional Digest,* Vol. 94, No. 2, February 2015.

They called for increased training and increased accountability. These arguments have framed the discussion on the militarization of police.[24]

On September 16, 2014, Henry "Hank" Johnson Jr. of Georgia's 4th congressional district introduced U.S. House Resolution (H.R.) 5478, the Stop Militarizing Law Enforcement Act, into the U.S. House of Representatives.[25] Sponsors of the bill cited the 2012 moratorium on weapons transfers, concerns about inappropriate police use of military-grade weapons against citizens, and the potential incentive for unnecessary use created by the requirement to use the equipment within one year of transfer. The bill required training and justification requirements, removed the counterdrug prioritization, and required LEAs to return surplus equipment. It also required LEAs to inform the community of property transfer, outlined items prohibited from transfer (including automatic weapons and those of .50 caliber or greater), eliminated the requirement of proof of weapons use within one year, ensured 100-percent accountability of controlled property, established a website to publicly document LEAs and equipment in the program, and did not allow any transfer of military-grade equipment among LEAs. The bill was referred to the House Armed Services Committee, where it died.

Later, on October 27, 2014, the ACLU sent a letter to the Secretary of Defense. Cosigned by a list of community partners, the letter requested a moratorium on the LESO program while the President's review was in progress.[26] The ACLU cited instances of LEAs being suspended from the program for missing weapons, educational institutions receiving LESO equipment, LEAs receiving weapons while being investigated by the U.S. Department of Justice (DoJ) for civil rights violations, and LEAs being unable to return LESO equipment to DoD as causes for concern about the program. The ACLU argued that a moratorium would allow DoD to assess the program without generating new concerns, much as the DLA-initiated moratorium on weapons transfers had accomplished in 2012.

On November 3, 2014, DoD implemented new strategies to improve the program's operation.[27] DLA began to coordinate information-sharing with DoJ to determine whether there were any open investigations on an LEA before transferring equipment. During a review of the Restricted Property List (103 federal supply classes [FSCs]), DoD invited DoJ to participate in verifying classes of equipment that were not appropriate for law enforcement operations. In addition to exchanging information with DoJ, DLA began notifying the Department of Homeland Security (DHS) of LEA suspensions and terminations from the LESO program, as DHS manages grant

---

[24] U.S. Senate Committee on Homeland Security and Governmental Affairs, "Oversight of Federal Programs for Equipping State and Local Law Enforcement," hearing transcript, September 9, 2014.

[25] H.R. 5478, Stop Militarizing Law Enforcement Act, 113th Congress, September 16, 2014.

[26] ACLU, 2014b.

[27] Executive Office of the President, "Review: Federal Support for Local Law Enforcement Equipment Acquisition," Washington, D.C., December 2014.

programs that provide equipment to LEAs. Finally, DoD began requiring states to attach certified training plans for property that required specialized training. These actions remain in effect today.[28]

On November 13, 2014, the House Subcommittee on Oversight and Investigations under the Committee on Armed Services held a hearing, "The Department of Defense Excess Property Program in Support of U.S. Law Enforcement Agencies: An Overview of DOD Authorities, Roles, Responsibilities, and Implementation of Section LESO of the 1997 National Defense Authorization Act." Witnesses and supporting stakeholders, including representatives from the Police Foundation, NTOA, Major County Sheriffs' Association, and the ACLU, made similar arguments to those outlined in the Senate hearing.[29] Recommendations included soliciting community members' input on the acquisition of equipment as part of the process, LEAs instituting publicly available policies governing the use of LESO property, requiring training in the use of this equipment, imposing a moratorium on the program, not expanding the scope of the program to include border security operations as cause for preference, eliminating the preference for counterdrug operations, and increasing accountability for the property transferred to LEAs.

In December 2014, the White House released its review of programs that support LEA equipment acquisition.[30] The review found that the bulk of equipment transferred was not tactical military equipment, though that category did constitute a substantial enough portion of the equipment to warrant action in controlling. It also found that programs like LESO do not have enough local community engagement, effective federal coordination and oversight, nor proper training requirements. Specific recommendations outlined in the White House review included

- developing a list of controlled and prohibited property
- requiring civilian review and authorization for receiving controlled property
- mandating training on use of the property and on protecting civil rights
- requiring after-action analysis reports for significant incidents using the equipment
- developing a database that includes information about controlled equipment that is transferred to LEAs.

---

[28] DLA, presentation to RAND by Michael Johnson, DLA J349, October 27, 2017.

[29] U.S. House of Representatives Committee Repository, "Hearing: The Department of Defense Excess Property Program in Support of U.S. Law Enforcement Agencies: An Overview of DOD Authorities, Roles, Responsibilities, and Implementation of Section 1033 of the 1997 National Defense Authorization Act," agenda, Washington, D.C., Subcommittee on Oversight and Investigations (Committee on Armed Services), November 13, 2014.

[30] Executive Office of the President, 2014.

Executive Order 13688

President Obama closely followed the Federal Review's recommendations when issuing EO 13688, "Federal Support for Local Law Enforcement Equipment Acquisition," on January 16, 2015.[31] The EO reiterated the importance of proper LEA training in the use of equipment as well as training in the protection of civil rights and civil liberties. It called for better cooperation and oversight in administering the program. The EO also established a "Law Enforcement Equipment Working Group" (also known as the Permanent Working Group [PWG]) that would make recommendations in five categories: equipment lists; policies, training, and protocols for controlled equipment; acquisition process for controlled equipment; transfer, sale, return, and disposal of controlled equipment; and oversight, compliance, and implementation. (The full content of EO 13688 appears in Appendix A.)

The PWG was cochaired by the Attorney General, the Secretary of Defense, and the Secretary of Homeland Security. Its members are the secretaries of the Treasury, Interior, and Education; the Administrator of General Services; the directors of the Domestic Policy Council, the Office of National Drug Control Policy, and the Office of Management and Budget; the assistants to the President for Intergovernmental Affairs and Public Engagement, and for Homeland Security and Counterterrorism; and the Assistant to the President and Chief of Staff of the Office of the Vice President.[32] The PWG was ordered to report to the President with recommendations.

At the direction of the cochairs, the PWG established subgroups consisting of PWG members or their designees. The executive director of the PWG determined the agenda, convened meetings, and supervised its work under the direction of the cochairs. The PWG was charged with engaging with external stakeholders—including appropriate state officials, law enforcement organizations, civil rights and civil liberties organizations, and academics—in developing the recommendations.

In the meantime, questions about police militarization were reignited in April of 2015 when Freddie Gray was injured in police custody in Baltimore.[33] While in custody, he sustained severe spinal injuries and died on April 19. Protests and riots broke out on April 18 and continued through May 3. As in Ferguson, the police response to the unrest was seen by some as heavy-handed, using unnecessary force.[34]

---

[31] White House Office of the Press Secretary, "Executive Order—Federal Support for Local Law Enforcement Equipment Acquisition," Executive Order 13688, President Barack Obama, Washington, D.C., January 16, 2015.

[32] PWG, *Recommendations Pursuant to the Executive Order 13688, Federal Support for Local Law Enforcement Equipment Acquisition*, May 2015.

[33] "Freddie Gray's Death in Police Custody—What We Know," BBC News, May 23, 2016.

[34] ACLU, "Statement on Freddie Gray and Police/Community Conflict in Baltimore," press release, April 28, 2015; Michael Gould-Wartofsky, "The Wars Come Home," *Huffington Post*, May 5, 2015.

In May 2015, the PWG issued a report pursuant to EO 13688 that included several program and policy recommendations to improve federal equipment acquisition programs. We highlight seven below:[35]

1. *Establishment of Federal Government–Wide Prohibited Equipment Lists.* The Prohibited Equipment List identified categories of equipment that LEAs would not be able to acquire via transfer from federal agencies or purchase using federally provided funds.
2. *Establishment of Federal Government–Wide Controlled Equipment Lists.* The Controlled Equipment List identified categories of equipment that LEAs, other than those solely serving schools with grades ranging from kindergarten through grade 12, could acquire if they provided additional information, certifications, and assurances. While inclusion on these lists would not preclude an LEA from using other funds for such acquisitions, the report urged LEAs to carefully consider the appropriateness of acquiring such equipment for their communities.
3. *Harmonization of Federal Acquisition Processes.* Under this recommendation, all federal equipment acquisition programs required LEAs that apply for controlled equipment to provide mandatory information in their application, including a detailed justification with a clear and persuasive explanation of the need for the controlled equipment; the availability of the requested controlled equipment to the LEA in its inventory or through other means; certifications that appropriate protocols and training requirements have been adopted; evidence of a civilian governing body's review and approval of, or concurrence with, the LEA's acquisition of the requested controlled equipment; and a statement affirming that the LEA has not been and is not in violation of civil rights and other statutes, regulations, or programmatic terms.
4. *Required Protocols and Training for LEAs that Acquire Controlled Equipment.* Under this recommendation, LEAs that acquire controlled equipment with federal resources would be required to adopt General Policing Standards, including community policing, constitutional policing, and community input and impact principles. It would also require LEAs to adopt Specific Controlled Equipment Standards on the appropriate use, supervision, evaluation, accountability, transparency, and operation of controlled equipment. LEAs would be required to train personnel on General Policing and Specific Controlled Equipment Standards on an annual basis.
5. *Required Information Collection and Retention for Controlled Equipment Use in Significant Incidents.* Under this recommendation, LEAs were required to collect and retain certain information when the LEA used controlled equipment in operations or actions that were deemed "Significant Incidents." LEAs were

[35] PWG, 2015.

also required to collect and retain information when allegations of unlawful or inappropriate police actions involving the use of controlled equipment triggered a federal compliance review of the LEA. Upon request, the LEA was required to provide this information to the federal agency that supplied the equipment/funds. This information would be made available to the community in accordance with the LEA's applicable policies and protocols.

6. *Approval for Third-Party Transfers or Sales.* Under this recommendation, LEAs were required to obtain approval from the federal agency that supplied the funds or equipment before selling or transferring controlled equipment. Third-party LEAs acquiring the controlled equipment had to provide the same information to the federal government. Sales or transfers to non-LEAs were restricted to certain types of controlled equipment that would not pose a great risk of danger or harm to the community if acquired by non-LEAs.
7. *Increased Federal Government Oversight and Compliance.* Under this recommendation, the federal government would expand its monitoring and compliance capabilities to ensure that LEAs acquiring controlled equipment adhered to protocols, training, information collection and retention, and other requirements proposed by the recommendations in the report. Additionally, the PWG would be charged with evaluating the Controlled and Prohibited Equipment Lists for additions and deletions, tracking controlled equipment purchased with federal resources, developing government-wide criteria for evaluating applications and conducting compliance reviews, and sharing information on sanctions and violations by LEA applicants.

President Obama accepted the PWG's recommendations, prohibited equipment lists took effect immediately, and the rest of the requirements listed were to start October 1, 2015. The PWG allowed a grace period, from October 2015 to March 2016, for LEAs to comply.

Multi-Agency Assessments and Adjustments

The DoJ released its after-action assessment of the events in Ferguson on September 3, 2015.[36] The report was critical of police response to the protests and riots. Highlighted in the report were findings that the display of tactical weapons and actions of the police were overly aggressive and inappropriate. The use of military-like weapons and deployment of military-like vehicles (e.g., armored personnel carriers) was found to be inappropriate and seemed to inflame tensions between the police and community. The assessment stated that the tactical deployment of this equipment during the day was inappropriate, though there were situations with sufficient cause for deployment. Making tactical vehicles visible as a means of crowd control was seen as threatening to

---

[36] Institute for Intergovernmental Research, *After-Action Assessment of the Police Response to the August 2014 Demonstrations in Ferguson, Missouri*, Community Oriented Policing Services, September 3, 2015.

citizens. In short, DoJ found that the police appeared militarized and that the appearance of militarization exacerbated the situation.[37]

On October 22, 2015, the *Defense Materiel Disposition Manual* was updated.[38] DoD revised the disposition process so that special programs (like the LESO program) can screen equipment in the first stage of the process along with other DoD components. As a result, in lieu of waiting until later in the 42-day process, special programs are now able to screen and request the property during the first 14 days, but DoD entities still have preference if an item is requisitioned at the same time.[39] This change facilitates greater efficiency and quicker disposition of excess property while still providing preference to internal reutilization by DoD components. (The disposition process is laid out in the next chapter.)

The 2016 NDAA was passed on November 25, 2015, and statute 10 U.S.C. 2576a was revised to align with changes outlined in sections 1051 and 1052. The changes added "border security operations" to the list of preferences (along with counterdrug and counterterrorism). In addition, LEAs were required to demonstrate that they had secured the support of a civilian oversight board for the transfer of controlled equipment. Further, LEAs were required to provide yearly training on the equipment. DLA was required to keep public records of LEAs that have acquired or have pending requests for controlled equipment.

In January 2016, GAO released another report, *Excess Personal Property: DOD Should Further Reassess the Priorities of Its Disposal Process.* GAO reported that the excess property transfer process allowed nonfederal agencies in special programs to access excess property before other federal non-LEA agencies.[40] While DLA had already adjusted its process so DoD agencies could access the property before special programs, other federal agencies (that were not law enforcement) could not access the property until later in the process. GAO argued that property bought with federal dollars should go to federal agencies first. Further, some DLA Disposition Services (DDS) sites had backlogs for turning in equipment, which meant that other DoD agencies had to store equipment at their expense. Disposition Services took steps to address these backlogs.

In February, the PWG released "Enhanced Criteria for Institutions of Higher Education (IHE) Applicants."[41] Under this document, IHE LEAs were required to show their civilian governing body's explicit review and approval before receiving con-

---

[37] None of equipment displayed during the Ferguson response was supplied through the LESO program.

[38] U.S. Department of Defense Manual 4160.21, *Defense Materiel Disposition Manual: Instructions for Hazardous Property and Other Special Processing Materiel*, Vol. 1–4, October 22, 2015.

[39] GAO, *Excess Personal Property: DOD Should Further Reassess the Priorities of Its Disposal Process*, GAO-16-44, January 29, 2016.

[40] GAO, 2016.

[41] PWG, "Enhanced Criteria for Institutions of Higher Education (IHE) Applicants," February 2016.

trolled property. The LEAs were also required to provide a detailed justification for why they needed the property. IHEs were also required to solicit community input and establish policies that ensure the equipment does not chill speech, disrupt the educational atmosphere, or foster a hostile climate toward students.

The LESO program received public attention again after the tragic events in Dallas, Texas. On July 7, 2016, a sniper targeted police officers working at a peaceful rally in downtown Dallas. Twelve officers were shot, and five were killed. Officers tried unsuccessfully to negotiate the surrender of the shooter. The five-hour standoff ended when Dallas police attached a bomb to a robot and detonated it near the shooter, who died in the blast. Several news reports erroneously indicated the robot was from the LESO program.[42]

Guidelines in Flux

The PWG provided updated recommendations to DLA in October 2016. Although most of the recommendations remained the same, the PWG came to a consensus that grenade launchers that fire nonlethal ammo, as well as vehicles that are not tactical in nature (e.g., pick-up trucks and SUVs), should be on the controlled list instead of the prohibited list. Riot helmets were removed from the controlled list after the PWG evaluated relevant factors like officer safety and community trust. The updated recommendations included a requirement that officers be trained on controlled equipment prior to use and to receive refresher training annually, which is not specifically directed in the legislative program guidance. The PWG reiterated that responsibility for how controlled equipment was used rested with the agency that took custody of the equipment.

As noted at the beginning of this chapter, section 1048 of the 2017 NDAA required DoD to contract with an FFRDC to evaluate the LESO program. According to the NDAA, the evaluation must include a review of the prohibited and controlled equipment lists; a review of the preferences and prioritization of counterdrug, counterterrorism, and border security operations; an analysis of whether DoD has bought the same type of equipment it has deemed excess in the same year; an evaluation of the type of information being collected by DLA and state coordinators; an outline of the reasons and occurrences of denial of equipment requests; and a review of the extent and reasons for LEA suspensions. RAND was hired to undertake that review and provide a comprehensive report to inform congressional staff considering changes to the program. (During the fiscal year [FY] 2017 NDAA deliberations, the House and Senate were unable to come to an agreement on the LESO program and, therefore, the

---

42 Alina Selyukh, "Bomb Robots: What Makes Killing in Dallas Different and What Happens Next?" NPR, July 8, 2016, Isabelle Taft, "Police Use of Robot to Kill Dallas Suspect Unprecedented, Experts Say," *Texas Tribune*, July 8, 2016; James Vincent, "Everything We Know About the Bomb Robot Used by Dallas Police," *The Verge*, July 8, 2016. DLA LESO data show that the Dallas County Sheriff's Department did acquire an explosive ordnance disposal bomb detection robot from the LESO program in April 2014, but the robot used to kill the suspect was not acquired through the program.

resulting language in Section 1048 of the FY 2017 NDAA represents a compromise, pending RAND's comprehensive evaluation.)

After the 2016 election, police advocates, such as the Fraternal Order of Police, predicted the new administration might rescind EO 13688.[43] A new bill was introduced in the House on January 10, 2017, and sent to the House Judiciary and Armed Services Committees. Titled "Protecting Lives Using Surplus Equipment Act of 2017," (U.S. House Resolution {H.R.] 426), the bill prohibited any regulation, rule, guidance, recommendation, or policy issued after May 15, 2015, that limited the transfer of excess property to LEAs.[44] It also prohibited federal agencies from using federal resources to implement a regulation, rule, guidance, recommendation, or policy that tried to limit transfers of equipment. Any property that was recalled or seized on or after May 15, 2015, would be returned, replaced, or reissued to LEAs at no cost to the agency. The bill was referred to the House Judiciary Subcommittee on Crime, Terrorism, Homeland Security, and Investigations on February 6, 2017, and to the House Armed Services Subcommittee on Readiness on February 21, 2017. At the time this report was published, no further progress was noted on this bill.

GAO Sting Operation

In July 2017, GAO released a report in which it described how GAO investigators were able to create a fictitious federal LEA, gain approval to use the LESO program, and obtain over 100 controlled items worth close to $1.2 million.[45] According to DLA officials, GAO investigators posed as a fictitious federal LEA in October 2015 and were not approved until January 2016 due to application problems that were flagged by LESO staff. LESO staff were eventually persuaded by a false website, created by GAO, and the application issues were resolved. DLA was notified in March of the vulnerability and immediately suspended the federal LEA special program.[46]

GAO concluded that DLA's internal controls at the time were insufficient to prevent the approval of a fraudulent enrollment application for a federal LEA. GAO also found that DLA officials did not consistently verify the quantity of approved items, that the officials did not consistently verify the identification of personnel authorized to accept excess property through the LESO program, and that effective fraud prevention and mitigation measures were not employed. GAO made four recommendations:

---

43 Fraternal Order of Police, "The Trump Administration: The First 100 Days," undated.

44 H.R. 426, Protecting Lives Using Surplus Equipment Act of 2017, 115th Congress, January 10, 2017.

45 GAO, *DOD Excess Property: Enhanced Controls Needed for Access to Excess Controlled Property*, GAO-17-532, July 18, 2017.

46 Prior to the GAO investigation, DLA had already commenced a manual verification process, developed a separate federal LEA program memorandum of agreement, established a new requirement for a federal LEA coordinator, set up required annual training, and identified a unique FBI-assigned National Crime Information-Center LEA Originating Agency Identifier number to use for future LEA verifications. The fictitious federal LEA was approved in the federal excess property acquisition system before the new controls had been implemented.

1. DLA should review and revise its procedures for verifying and approving federal LEA enrollments.
2. DLA should ensure on-site officials request and verify valid identification of individuals authorized to receive equipment.
3. DLA should issue guidance to on-site officials to verify the type and quantity of approved equipment prior to transfer.
4. DLA should conduct a fraud risk assessment with an ultimate goal to implement appropriate internal control activities to mitigate risk, consistent with GAO's Fraud Risk Framework.

DLA is in the process of implementing the GAO-recommended actions.

We learned in interviews with GAO and DLA officials that the GAO audit, which was mandated in the 2016 NDAA, was to focus on state and local LEAs; however, investigators noted a vulnerability in the vetting process for federal LEAs and altered their focus. GAO officials expressed an interest in focusing further on the LESO program in other areas, including LEA vetting; disposal of controlled equipment; denials through the application process (program enrollment versus requisition denials); causes of suspensions, particularly inventory control violations; verification of program requirements, specifically the number of sworn officers; potential conflicts of interest associated with the appointment of state coordinators who approve both enrollments and requisitions; and in-state controlled equipment transfer program compliance.

Executive Order 13809

On August 28, 2017, President Trump issued EO 13809, "Restoring State, Tribal, and Local Law Enforcement's Access to Life-Saving Equipment and Resources," which revoked President Obama's EO 13688. In revoking EO 13688, the Attorney General cited two 2017 *American Economic Journal* articles as justification that the DoD excess equipment provided through the LESO program reduces crime. (The full content of EO 13809 appears in Appendix B.)

In the first article,[47] "Police Officer on the Frontline or a Soldier? The Effect of Police Militarization on Crime," the authors sought to answer whether providing surplus military equipment to local police affects crime rates and, if so, through what mechanism (i.e., how precisely does this equipment cause the effect). They concluded that military aid reduces street-level crime, that the program is cost-effective, and that there is evidence in favor of a deterrence mechanism. The authors found that a 10-percent increase in military aid is associated with a decrease of 5.9 crimes per 100,000 residents.

However, in our considered opinion, the correlation is likely spurious. First, the authors implausibly assert that the previous year's level of military spending drives the

[47] Vincenzo Bove and Evelina Gavrilova, "Police Officer on the Frontline or a Soldier? The Effect of Police Militarization on Crime," *American Economic Journal: Economic Policy*, Vol. 9, No. 3, 2017, pp. 1–18.

amount of equipment available for transfer in the following year. Second, the authors cannot explain how the equipment transfers affect crime. They hypothesize that deterrence is the primary effect, but this is difficult to justify, given that most transfers do not involve crime-fighting materials and instead more directly contribute to overall officer safety and readiness. Moreover, most transfers offer financial relief to small LEAs by providing equipment that would otherwise be unaffordable or would be general consumables (e.g., protective clothing, hand tools, emergency medical supplies), as opposed to crime-fighting materials.

In the second article, "Peacekeeping Force: Effects of Providing Tactical Equipment to Local Law Enforcement," the authors sought to test whether having military equipment leads police to be more aggressive toward citizens.[48] They use citizen complaints, offender deaths, and assaults on officers as indicators of aggressive policing. They concluded that excess military equipment has generally positive effects: reduced citizen complaints, reduced assaults on officers, increased drug crime arrests, and no increases in offender deaths. One weakness of the study, however, is that the primary data source on citizen complaints is collected manually from annual reports. How comparable across jurisdictions and how complete within jurisdictions these records are is unclear.

Where to Now?

This history shows how the LESO program has evolved over time—in response to statutory changes, congressional inquiry, executive orders, and GAO findings. It has faced public scrutiny and sits at the center of a debate surrounding police militarization. Although program changes stemming from congressional oversight have been implemented with apparent fidelity, LESO is simply not designed nor equipped to answer questions about the appropriateness of transferring excess DoD equipment to LEAs. In short, *LESO is fundamentally in the business of logistics and is ill-suited to resolve contentious issues about the nature of policing in our democracy. Over the course of this research, we find this to be the central issue*, and we will return to it throughout this report. First, however, we discuss the process LESO follows to transfer excess property.

---

[48] Matthew C. Harris, Jinseong Park, Donald J. Bruce, and Matthew N. Murray, "Peacekeeping Force: Effects of Providing Tactical Equipment to Local Law Enforcement," *American Economic Journal: Economic Policy*, Vol. 3, No. 3, 2017, pp. 291–313.

CHAPTER TWO

Excess Property and LESO Program Processes

In this chapter, we describe the processes that DLA uses to transfer and dispose of excess DoD property and, specifically, how property is transferred to LEAs. This chapter will help the reader understand the controls in place and the time pressures that the program is under. It should also clarify the care taken to ensure the process runs as efficiently as possible.

DoD Excess Property Transfer and Disposal Time Line

The transfer process starts when one of the military services or components determines that a piece of equipment is no longer necessary. Whenever this happens (on a revolving basis), the equipment is entered into the DoD supply system and assigned a demilitarization code. DLA validates the code when the property is turned in. The codes indicate whether the property is available for reuse with or without restriction, such as removal of any sensitive technology, classified components, or trade security control.[1] Once processed by DLA Disposition Services, the equipment is redistributed for (1) reuse inside DoD, (2) transfer to organizations through special programs (e.g., LESO), (3) transfer to other federal agencies, (4) donation to state and local agencies or other organizations other than LEAs, or (5) sale or destruction if it remains unclaimed.

Figure 2.1 provides a time line of the disposal process. LESO is one of the "special programs" mentioned on the left side of the time line.

In the chart, *reutilize* refers to the first 14 days, when DLA Disposition Services posts information about the property on its website for Reutilization, Transfer, Donation (RTD). During this stage, DoD services and components can screen equipment at the same time as special programs. In this stage, DLA disposes of the majority of its excess property (about 90 percent). Although LEAs can screen and request property during this phase, property is not distributed to them if a DoD service or component requests the identical item during the first 14 days.

---

1 DoD Manual 4160.28-V2, *Defense Demilitarization: Demilitarization Coding*, June 7, 2011.

Figure 2.1
DoD's Item Disposal Process

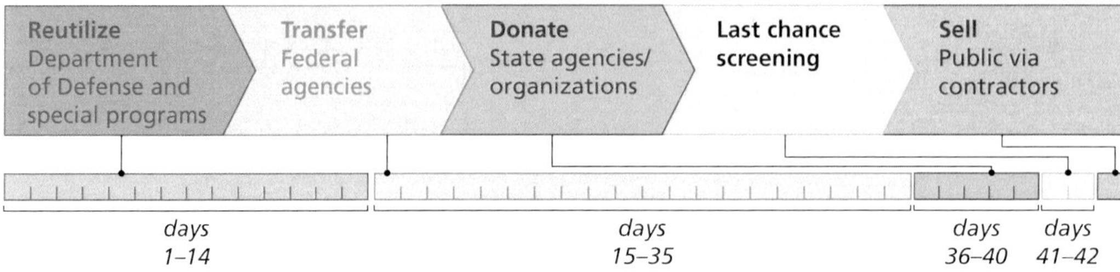

SOURCES: GAO analysis of Defense Logistics Agency (DLA) data; GAO, "Excess Personal Property: DOD Should Further Reassess the Priorities of Its Disposal Process," GAO-16-44, January 29, 2016.
RAND *RR2464-2.1*

Time is central in the LESO process. After items are posted on the RTD website, LEAs have two weeks to submit a request. The goal is to move equipment quickly and avoid storage. LEAs, therefore, have an incentive to monitor available LESO items avidly; more-participative LEAs are more likely to get items. LEAs cannot prerequest items, but there is an exception for two types of equipment: aircraft and tactical vehicles.[2] As of April 2017, there was a waiting list of preapproved LEAs awaiting the availability of helicopters, fixed-wing aircraft, and MRAP vehicles.

Aside from LEAs, other designated special programs can screen excess property inventories and requisition equipment during the first 14 days. These other special programs include Foreign Military Sales, U.S. Department of Agriculture (USDA) firefighters, humanitarian assistance programs (HAPs), the Military Affiliate Radio System (MARS), Civil Air Patrols, senior Reserve Officers' Training Corps (ROTC) units, DoD or service museums, and Computers for Learning. Note that *federal* LEAs, such as the Drug Enforcement Administration (DEA), Customs and Border Protection (CBP), and the Federal Bureau of Investigation (FBI), can also compete in the LESO program at this time.

Next in Figure 2.1 is the word *Transfer*. Transfer refers to the next 21 days (days 15 to 35) after DoD, special programs, and federal LEAs have screened the excess property. Excess property that is still available is offered to all other federal agencies. During the transfer phase, both federal and nonfederal entities may view excess property on the GSA website. DoD components are still able to request property during this stage. For example, federal civil agencies—including the Forest Service, Veterans Affairs, and Agriculture—continue to have access to excess property during this stage.

The third stage (days 36 to 40) is *Donation*. During these five days, excess property is declared surplus and donated to state and municipal governments or other qual-

[2] DoD defines *tactical vehicles* as vehicles having military characteristics resulting from military research and development processes, designed primarily for use by forces in the field in direct connection with, or support of, combat or tactical operations.

ified organizations through the Federal Surplus Personal Property Donation Program. Other qualified recipients include public agencies and nonprofit educational, public health, and veterans' organizations that have been approved by the Small Business Administration. The last two days of the 42-day cycle provide all eligible recipients a final chance to screen and request surplus property before it is sold or destroyed.

The fourth and final phase is *Sell*, where unclaimed, usable property that is determined viable for sale is sold through commercial contracts. Those items not viable for sale are scrapped or disposed of.[3]

State Coordinators

Before entering the LESO process, LEAs must work with a gubernatorial-appointed state coordinator, who approves an LEA's application to the program. State coordinators are employed in different offices in different states. Some are sworn officers, others are LEA employees, and others have no law enforcement background. Some are civilians employed by their state's office of emergency services or by their state's version of the GSA (i.e., an agency that handles state governmental property). State coordinators are required to attend an annual training seminar.

This training is mandated in Title 10 of U.S. Code 380, which stipulates that the "Secretary of Defense, in cooperation with the Attorney General, shall conduct an annual briefing of law enforcement personnel of each State regarding information, training, technical support, and equipment and facilities available to civilian law enforcement personnel from the Department of Defense."[4] Additionally, in accordance with 10 U.S.C. 2576a, state coordinators are to ensure that the LEA recipients in their state, on an annual basis, certify that annual training is provided "to relevant personnel on the maintenance, sustainment, and appropriate use of controlled property."[5]

Once approved, the state coordinator is required to enter into written agreement with each of the state's LEAs. This agreement is called the LESO-approved State Plan of Operation,[6] and it is intended to ensure that LEAs acknowledge the terms, conditions, and limitations applicable to the property transferred. Moreover, each state coordinator is guided by a signed MOA that mirrors DLA instructions and provides guidance to state coordinators on how the program is to be managed. DLA maintains

---

3 GAO, 2016.

4 U.S. Code, Title 10, Section 380, Enhancement of Cooperation with Civilian Law Enforcement Officials.

5 10 U.S.C. 2576a.

6 DLA (2016) provides a template for a state plan of operations between a state and an LEA. The plan must be signed by each chief LEA official participating in the LESO program. The plan defines the roles and responsibilities of program participation and is the agreement between the state coordinator and each participating LEA head.

a comprehensive website that contains all guides, instructions, and forms to administer a state program.

Once an LEA application is approved by the state coordinator, the LESO program makes the final determination on whether an LEA can participate. One key issue that LESO looks for is whether the agency is truly "law enforcement." LESO-eligible LEAs must be government agencies whose primary function is the enforcement of applicable federal, state, and local laws and whose compensated officers have the powers of arrest and apprehension.

Registration Process

To participate in the program, LEAs must follow a triple registration process. Participants are required to register in three systems: the Account Management and Provisioning Service (AMPS), RTD, and the Federal Excess Property Management Information System (FEPMIS).

- AMPS is used to manage access to government systems. Participants initially register in this system to gain permissions to request equipment. The AMPS registration is a three-step process.
- RTD allows users to search and request property; this site is available to all designated and approved screeners, and each user must register with an approved AMPS identification.
- FEPMIS is the inventory control system. LEAs are responsible for completing an annual inventory and reporting the results to state coordinators and federal program administrators using their FEPMIS account. LEAs who fail to complete the annual inventory requirement face suspension.

After obtaining approval, each participating LEA receives a unique Department of Defense Activity Address Code (DODAAC), which is a six-position code that identifies a DoD unit, activity, or organization that has the authority to requisition, contract for, receive, have custody of, issue, or ship DoD assets. The DODAAC is included on DoD Form 1348-1a, which is the primary method for processing property. In addition to the DODAAC, the form contains other mandatory fields, including the National Stock Number (NSN), nomenclature, unit of issue, quantity, demilitarization code, condition code, unit price, and a disposal authorization code.

Reviews of Equipment Requests

Once admitted to the program, an LEA can begin requesting equipment. Requests go first to the state coordinator, who can approve or reject the request. Coordinators frequently work with the LEA to improve the application (e.g., writing a better justification for acquisition) before it is passed on to LESO. (Requisitions rejected by the state coordinator are not sent to LESO.) When requesting controlled tactical vehicles, LEAs must complete an extra step, referred to as the "Executive Order Request" form. Tactical vehicles include armored vehicles, cargo trucks, dump trucks, wreckers, truck vans, and high-mobility multipurpose wheeled vehicles (HMMWVs). Any request for tactical equipment must be approved by the state coordinator and LESO.[7]

In addition, a civilian governing body's review and approval are required before requisitioning controlled equipment. For police departments, this review and approval reside with the mayor's office or city council. For sheriff's departments, the review and approval come in the form of a written notice to the county board of supervisors. Moreover, some states (e.g., New Jersey, Montana) require passage of a resolution before approving any requests for controlled equipment or have promulgated specific legislation that mandates additional controls or notifications of controlled equipment acquisitions and holdings.

In determining whether to approve a request, LESO relies on a set of written policies. For instance, one policy states that an LEA should not have more than one item (e.g., a weapon) per sworn officer and no more than one vehicle per three sworn officers.[8] In addition to these policies, LESO staff consult with DoJ for guidance related to LEAs that are under DoJ investigation.[9] Ultimately, however, LESO is the decision-making authority.

If more than one LEA applies for the same piece of equipment, we were told that, in most cases, the first LEA application to arrive at LESO and be approved is awarded the equipment. That is, the process is first come, first served, as long as the application is in order.

Equipment Deliveries and Training

If a requisition is approved, the LEA must retrieve the equipment or pay for shipment. Some state coordinators assess handling fees on LEAs. Louisiana, for example,

---

[7] The steps described here follow guidance from EO 13688. There are still unknowns after EO 13809 (Executive Office of the President, Executive Order 13809, "Restoring State, Tribal, and Local Law Enforcement's Access to Lifesaving Equipment and Resources," August 28, 2017). In accordance with the EO 13809 Implementation Plan, "LESO will return to previous procedures requiring further justification paperwork for "High Profile" property (Aircraft, Armored Vehicles, Weapons). Cargo Trucks/Riot & Breaching equipment will not require additional justification/paperwork."

[8] Specifically, tactical vehicles (HMMWV, MRAP, personnel carriers), where one is allowed for every three officers; and small arms (M16, M14, Glock, M1911, .38 Special), where one is allowed for each officer (except M14, where the allowance is one for every two officers).

[9] For a review of some of its work on the conduct of LEAs, see DoJ, 2017.

charges $15,000 for delivery of an MRAP vehicle, $10,000 for an aircraft, $2,000 for an HMMWV, $100 for a rifle, and $50 for a pistol. States that charge handling fees to their LEAs use this revenue to defray the costs of the coordinator's office. Other states support the process through general funding.

When an LEA receives equipment, it is recorded in LESO's inventory system, or FEPMIS. The LEA must pay all costs to operate and maintain the equipment. In addition, LEAs are responsible for training on controlled equipment. LEA training must include scenario-based training that combines both constitutional and community-policing principles with equipment-specific training. LEAs must also certify that they maintain a training plan and safety standards that cover the use of all requested equipment. LEAs must retain at least three years of training records documenting officers who were trained and must provide a copy of records on request.

Reviewing FEPMIS, we found that LEAs at all levels use the program but that the vast majority are state LEAs. The majority of the property being issued to LEAs is noncontrolled property without military attributes or appearance. This includes items such as office furniture and equipment, kitchen supplies, exercise equipment, field equipment (blankets, backpacks, tents), medical supplies (tourniquets, first-aid kits, body bags), tools, generators, heavy equipment (trailers, forklifts, earth movers, utility vehicles), and fencing.[10] DLA guidelines allow LEAs to obtain excess military property that is not exclusively related to law enforcement activities as long as LEAs provide justification and the state coordinator approves.[11]

Equipment Transfers and Losses

When an LEA no longer wants a piece of LESO-controlled equipment, it must notify LESO, which will transfer the equipment to another LEA or ask the LEA to return the item. An LEA must also inform LESO if an item is lost or destroyed. If an LEA loses a weapon, the LEA is suspended from the program and must submit an acceptable corrective action plan to restore participation. As we discuss in Chapter Three, repeated equipment loss may result in an LEA's termination from the program, including an obligation to return all remaining LESO-provided equipment.

Compliance Reviews

A regular Program Compliance Review (PCR) is required at both the federal and state levels. The federal-level PCR is conducted every two years by DDS LESO to assess

[10] Executive Office of the President, 2014.

[11] DLA, 2016.

whether federal LEAs are complying with the terms of the program. The state-level PCR can be conducted anytime throughout the year by state officials.

State-level PCR teams complete an annual physical inventory of items received by the subject agency, review all documentation associated with program administration and accountability, and assess whether the LEA is compliant with terms and conditions of the program. The intent of each PCR is to verify the disposition of 20 percent of the LESO-provided weapons held by LEAs in the state. Conditional on visiting an LEA, the LESO PCR team inventories 100 percent of the LEA's LESO-provided weapons, vehicles, and aircraft and, at a minimum, 10 percent of all other LESO-provided property.

Federal-level LESO PCR reports that were conducted over a yearlong period for 24 states and the Virgin Islands were reviewed by RAND researchers. These 25 LESO PCR visits encompassed 586 total LEAs visited and verified. The large majority of LEAs were found to be in compliance with virtually all inventory accounted for. A total of 23,453 pieces of equipment were audited; 23,236 were accounted for (99.1 percent). The PCR process is regarded by DLA, state coordinators, and LEAs as necessary to maintain the integrity of the program and identify noncompliance and/or other areas of concern on a recurring basis.

CHAPTER THREE

Transfers, Losses, Suspensions, Terminations, and Rebuys

In this chapter, we turn to the strictly quantitative aspects of the LESO program that we analyzed. These aspects include (1) the types of equipment transferred and to whom, (2) losses, suspensions, and terminations, and (3) rebuys of excess equipment. Chapter Four will summarize our stakeholder interviews, while Chapter Five will summarize our survey results.

Types of Equipment Transferred and to Whom

Since its inception, the LESO program has distributed equipment valued at more than $6 billion. This equipment falls into two distinct categories: controlled equipment remains the property of DoD in perpetuity until returned to DLA, and noncontrolled equipment passes to LEA ownership and drops off the DoD books after one year. A third type of equipment, prohibited equipment, was, as the name indicates, prohibited for transfer—according to EO 13688, an Obama-era executive order.

During our study, President Trump issued EO 13809, which revoked EO 13688. The LESO program, therefore, is undergoing revision in accordance with EO 13809, with a target rollout in October 2018. Preliminary discussions with LESO indicate intentions to revert back to DoD's 132 previously prohibited federal supply classes, which would resume transfers of tracked armored vehicles and bayonets, as had occurred prior to EO 13688.[1] This equipment would still be categorized as "controlled," and therefore ownership would be retained by DoD.

The items listed in List 3.1 are those included in the prohibited list that had resulted from the Obama-era EO.

Items shown in List 3.2 are referred to as *Executive Order–controlled*, or *EO-controlled*. EO-controlled items are a subset of controlled items. There are also DoD-controlled items. In both cases, these are military-specific items such as night-vision goggles, robots, communication equipment, and binoculars. The items in List 3.2 were controlled in the Obama era.

---

1 DLA, "Executive Order 13809 Implementation Plan," October 2017.

List 3.1
EO 13688 Prohibited Equipment

Tracked armored vehicles
Weaponized aircraft, vessels, and vehicles of any kind
Firearms of .50 caliber or higher
Ammunition of.50 caliber or higher
Grenade launchers
Bayonets
Camouflage uniforms

SOURCE: EO 13688, p. 3.

List 3.2
EO 13688 Controlled Equipment

Manned aircraft, fixed wing
Manned aircraft, rotary wing
Unmanned aerial vehicles
Armored vehicles, wheeled
Tactical vehicles, wheeled
Command and control vehicles
Specialized firearms and ammunition under .50 caliber
Explosives and pyrotechnics
Breaching apparatus
Riot batons
Riot helmets
Riot shields

SOURCE: EO 13688, pp. 36–37.

List 3.3 lists DoD-controlled equipment. These items include aircraft (manned, unmanned, fixed- and rotary-wing), vehicles (tactical, armored, and command and control), and specialized tactical weapons and gear. The items in List 3.3 continue to be controlled today. The only difference between the EO-controlled items in List 3.2, from the Obama era, and the DoD-controlled items in List 3.3 is EO 13688's control of explosives and pyrotechnics.

List 3.3
DoD-Controlled Equipment

Manned aircraft
Fixed- or rotary-wing aircraft
Unmanned aerial vehicles
Wheeled armored vehicles
Wheeled tactical vehicles
Command and control vehicles
Specialized firearms and ammunition under .50 caliber (excluded firearms and ammunition for service-issued weapons)
Breaching apparatus
Riot batons
Riot helmets
Riot shields

SOURCE: DDS, "Controlled Property Definition," fact sheet, April 18, 2017.

Uncontrolled items—the final type of equipment that can be requisitioned—include, as noted in the previous chapter, items such as desks, computer equipment, first aid kits, and tools.

Delving into quality and value, Table 3.1 uses FEPMIS data to break out the number and value of items in LEA possession. As the table shows, LEAs use the LESO program for uncontrolled property more than for controlled property, in terms of quantity. However, in terms of value, controlled property represents the significant majority (82 percent). Additionally, while EO 13688 designated all property in List 3.1 as prohibited, and while there is no evidence of prohibited transfers after the executive order, there are numerous prohibited items currently being held by LEAs. During our interviews of LEA points of contact, we learned that after EO 13688 was issued in January 2015 and the prohibited items list was updated in May 2015, some LEAs were left with equipment that was, at that point, prohibited from transfer and use. Some of these LEAs simply took the affected equipment out of circulation and placed it in a secure warehouse or storage location, awaiting final disposition. The equipment included riot gear, bayonets, camouflaged clothing, and personal protective equipment. However, following EO 13809, these items are no longer considered prohibited.

From laptops to rifles, 7,179 unique types of items were transferred to LEAs through the LESO program in FYs 2015 to 2017. However, of the property currently held by LEAs, just the top 20 types of items (in terms of value) make up 80 percent of the nearly $1.9 billion total value of all transfers. Table 3.2 shows that 14 of the top 20 types of currently held items by value are vehicles, including trucks and aircraft. MRAPs—specifically, 849 of them—make up 31 percent of the total value of all LESO items currently held by LEAs.

The top 20 types of currently held items by quantity are different. As shown in Table 3.3, magazine cartridges are the single most frequent items transferred through the LESO program. While other frequently transferred items include 5.56- and 7.62-millimeter rifles, the majority of the top 20 types of items currently held, by quan-

Table 3.1
Current Property Held by LEAs: Quantity and Value, by Class (FY 2016 dollars)

Property Class	Quantity (percentage of total)	Acquisition Value (percentage of total)
Grand total	*1,567,635 (100%)*	*$ 1,888,559,339 (100%)*
Controlled	666,821 (42.54%)	$ 1,548,498,226 (81.99%)
Prohibited	5,591 (0.36%)	$ 417,772 (0.02%)
Uncontrolled	895,223 (57.11%)	$ 339,643,341 (17.98%)

SOURCE: Data provided by LESO to RAND.

NOTE: Uncontrolled items remain on the LEA FEPMIS inventory for only one year, while controlled items remain on the FEPMIS inventory until returned to DLA.

Table 3.2
Current Property Held by LEAs: Top 20, by Value (FY 2016 dollars, DoD purchase price)

Property Description	Quantity	Value ($)
Grand total	*1,567,635*	*1,888,559,339*
Mine resistant vehicle	849	582,950,991
Truck, utility	5,608	284,975,379
Aircraft, rotary wing	9	144,200,000
Aircraft, fixed wing	18	123,321,000
Helicopter, utility	95	87,612,794
Helicopter, observation	313	37,295,725
Helicopter, search and rescue	8	28,853,000
Rifle, 5.56 millimeter	64,689	27,834,376
Truck tractor	172	23,099,425
Combat/assault/tactical wheeled vehicles	97	21,896,158
Truck, armored	302	19,647,847
Image intensifier, night vision	5,141	19,547,195
Helicopter, flight trainer	23	19,168,200
Visible and invisible light communication equipment	112	19,040,000
Truck, cargo	218	15,447,152
Comms, equip.	3	15,000,000
Mk3mod0 knife	77	13,919,644
Unmanned vehicle	72	12,857,216
Sight, thermal	1,346	12,362,899
Airplane, cargo-transport	15	11,753,875

SOURCE: Data provided by LESO to RAND.
NOTE: Value based on DoD purchase price.

tity, are ordinary items such as field packs, first-aid kits, and clothing. The 5.56-millimeter rifles are the only items that appear in both Table 3.2 and Table 3.3.

In regard to uncontrolled property, the most frequent transfers of this type are shown in Table 3.4. While reflex sights are the single most common items among the currently held types of uncontrolled property, first-aid equipment and clothing are also high on the list.

Table 3.3
Current Property Held by LEAs: Top 20, by Quantity (FY 2016 dollars)

Property Description	Quantity	Value ($)
Grand total	*1,567,635*	*1,888,559,339*
Magazine, cartridge	159,803	17,890
Rifle, 5.56 millimeter	64,689	27,834,376
Field pack	52,026	274,879
Sight, reflex	47,385	3,418,940
Tourniquet, nonpneumatic	35,183	9,246
Flashlight	21,095	236,559
First aid kit, individual	20,054	38,596
Light, chemiluminescent	18,811	11,440
Bandage, gauze	17,999	1,787
Bandage, gauze, impregnated	17,095	4,105
Chest, ammunition	16,466	2,076
Wire, electrical	16,363	2,168
Rifle, 7.62 millimeter	14,791	2,138,990
Dressing, first aid, field	13,633	203
Goggles, ballistic	11,627	5,025
Jacket, cold weather	11,585	44,545
Shirt, cold weather	11,462	33,104
Dressing, compression	11,289	155
Illuminator, infrared	10,584	4,776,325
Socks	10,500	119

SOURCE: Data provided by LESO to RAND.
NOTE: Value based on DoD purchase price.

The most frequently transferred types of controlled property that are currently held by LEAs, as shown in Table 3.5, are rifles, handguns, and magazines. Goggles, sights, and spectacles have also been commonly transferred to LEAs.

Table 3.6 shows that smaller LEAs represent a large share of the program's users, which is unsurprising given the prevalence of smaller agencies in general.[2] While larger

[2] Forty-eight percent of LEAs (more than 12,000 LEAs nationwide) employed fewer than ten officers, according to the U.S. Department of Justice Office of Justice Programs, Bureau of Justice Statistics, *Law Enforcement Management and Administrative Statistics (LEMAS) Survey, 1987–2013*, NCJ-248677, May 2015.

Table 3.4
Current Uncontrolled Property Held by LEAs: Top 20, by Quantity (FY 2016 dollars)

Property Description	Quantity	Value ($)
Grand total	*783,404*	*331,123,023*
Sight, reflex	47,385	3,418,940
Tourniquet, nonpneumatic	35,183	9,246
Flashlight	21,095	236,559
First aid kit, individual	20,054	38,596
Light, chemiluminescent	18,811	11,440
Bandage, gauze	17,999	1,787
Bandage, gauze, impregnated	17,095	4,105
Chest, ammunition	16,466	2,076
Wire, electrical	16,363	2,168
Dressing, first aid, field	13,633	203
Dressing, compression	11,289	155
Illuminator, infrared	10,584	4,776,325
Socks	10,500	119
First aid kit, universal	10,427	13,300
Screw, tapping	9,477	3
Multi-tool, folding, pocket	8,790	7,537
Liner, wet weather poncho	7,592	6,584
Strap, tie down, electrical components	6,439	292
Undershirt, man's	6,341	379
Module, trauma	6,106	1,801

SOURCE: Data provided by LESO to RAND.

NOTE: Value based on DoD purchase price.

agencies tend to have more LESO-provided equipment (or more-expensive equipment), other participation indicators, such as those expressed on a percentage basis, show a uniformity across LEAs regardless of size. About a third of the smallest LEAs have acquired vehicles from LESO—not too dissimilar from the 47 to 51 percent of LEAs in the larger categories; in fact, a higher percentage of small LEAs hold LESO transferred weapons. Only with aircraft do we see a bias toward possession by larger agencies.

Table 3.5
Current Controlled Property Held by LEAs: Top 20, by Quantity (FY 2016 dollars)

Property Description	Quantity	Value ($)
Grand total	*671,852*	*1,548,914,244*
Magazine, cartridge	159,803	17,890
Rifle, 5.56 millimeter	64,689	27,834,376
Field pack	52,026	274,879
Rifle, 7.62 millimeter	14,791	2,138,990
Goggles, ballistic	11,627	5,025
Goggles, industrial	9,998	15,030
Buttstock, subassembly	9,849	1,497
Canteen, water	9,140	459
Intrenching tool, hand	8,184	14,986
Pistol, caliber .45, automatic	7,305	428,877
Spectacles, industrial	6,934	6,697
Sight, rear	6,285	26,905
Modular sleep system	6,205	99,959
Truck, utility	5,608	284,975,379
Spectacle kit, interchangeable component eyeshield	5,450	2,168
Sleeping bag	5,380	16,152
Cleaning kit, gun	5,213	8,004
Spectacles, ballistic and laser protective	5,212	2,993
Carrier, intrenching tool	5,179	1,006
Cover, water canteen	4,414	196

SOURCE: Data provided by LESO to RAND.
NOTE: Value based on DoD purchase price.

Table 3.6 also provides information on recent activity organized by LEA size. Only 20 percent of LEAs currently holding LESO equipment had a request filled in the most recent period, with no clear relationship between size and likelihood of using the program in that year or number of requests filled. Indeed, smaller agencies can be the most-active users of LESO, as indicated by the small LEAs (those with fewer than 25 officers) that had 525 requests filled in the past year.

On the topic of MRAPs, as Table 3.7 shows, a third of MRAPs were acquired by LEAs with fewer than 50 sworn officers and close to two-thirds by those with fewer

Table 3.6
Participation by LEA Size, as of FY 2016

	LEA Size (number of officers)					
	Fewer than 25	25–49	50–99	100–249	250 or More	Unknown
Number of LEAs	4,229	1,465	891	638	408	117
Dollar value of holdings (mean/median)	$100,534 /$4,855	$230,065 /$41,061	$359,604 /$84,290	$433,426 /$121,696	$1,517,955/ $340,328	$2,468,472 /$34,065
LEAs with vehicles	1,452 (34%)	636 (51%)	456 (50%)	317 (50%)	192 (47%)	32 (27%)
LEAs with weapons	3,203 (75%)	1,059 (72%)	615 (69%)	433 (68%)	346 (60%)	26 (22%)
LEAs with aircraft	9 (0.2%)	19 (1%)	19 (2%)	41 (6%)	82 (20%)	5 (4%)
LEAs with requisitions June 2015–May 2016	690 (16%)	352 (24%)	244 (27%)	64 (10%)	151 (37%)	25 (21%)
Requisitions filled, June 2015–May 2015 (mean/median)	19/6	18/5	20/4	24/7	47/13	39/7
Requisitions by most-active LEAs June 2015–May 2015	525	234	222	333	601	406

SOURCE: Data provided by LESO to RAND.

NOTE: Values based on FY 2016 Federal Logistics Data on Mobile Media (FEDLOG) figures.

than 100 officers. As with the results in Table 3.6, the number of smaller LEAs receiving MRAPs is unsurprising given that 88 percent of LEAs in 2013 had fewer than 50 sworn officers.[3]

We turn now to how requisitions were split among local, state, federal, and tribal LEAs: Between FYs 2015 and 2017, over 2.2 million uncontrolled items worth nearly

Table 3.7
Size Distribution of LEAs Receiving MRAPs, as of FY 2016

Number of Officers	Number of MRAPs	Percentage of all MRAPs
24 or fewer	76	11
25–49	155	22.5
50–99	202	29.4
100–249	168	24.4
250 or more	87	12.6

SOURCE: Data provided by LESO to RAND.

NOTE: Values based on FY 2016 FEDLOG figures.

[3] U.S. Department of Justice Office of Justice Programs, Bureau of Justice Statistics, 2015.

$1.2 billion and over 3,000 controlled items worth nearly $775 million were transferred to 2,790 state LEAs (1,332 of which received controlled items), 174 federal LEAs (17 of which received controlled items), and 22 tribal LEAs (13 of which received controlled items).

As shown in Figure 3.1, state LEAs received the majority of LESO equipment in both quantity and value. This is especially true for controlled items, for which states hold 97 percent of this class of property by value. Federal LEAs have received 11 percent of the total property and 18 percent of the total value of LESO equipment. Of the property disbursed to federal LEAs, the majority (by quantity and value) is uncontrolled, whereas the majority of the property disbursed to state LEAs (by quantity and value) is controlled. Tribal LEAs receive only 1 percent of property in terms of value and quantity.

Figure 3.1 shows that the amount of controlled property held by all LEAs (state, federal, and tribal) is not distributed evenly. For controlled property, 1 percent of all LEAs hold 25 percent of the total quantity and 30 percent of the total value. In fact, just five LEAs have 20 percent of the value of controlled items. There is a similar story for uncontrolled property: Just 10 LEAs control 36 percent of the quantity and 20 percent of the value. For uncontrolled property, 10 percent of LEAs receive 73 percent of the items.

Additionally, nearly half of the quantity of controlled property is transferred to three states (California, Texas, and Georgia), while half the value goes to seven states

Figure 3.1
Distribution of Property (and Value) Distributed to State, Federal, and Tribal LEAs, FY 2015–2017

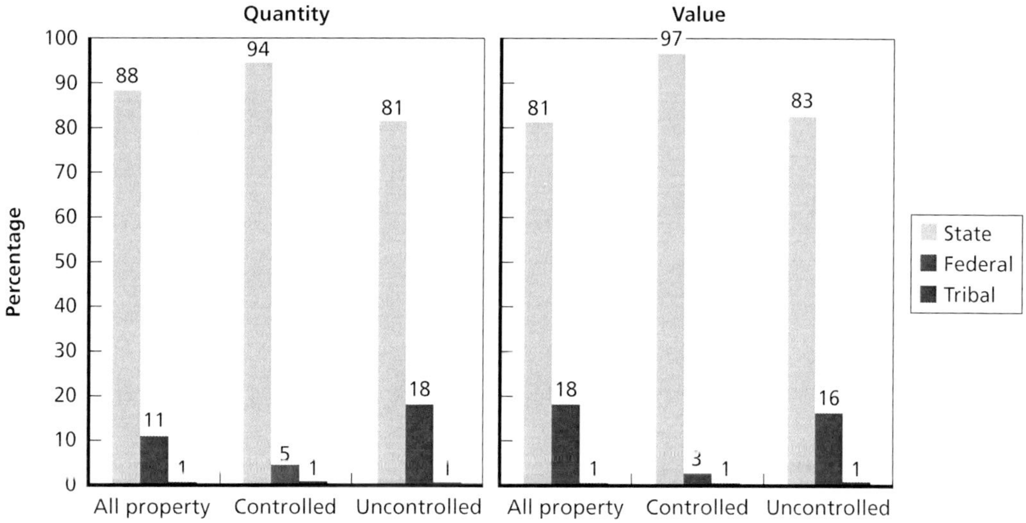

SOURCE: Data provided by LESO to RAND.
RAND *RR2464-3.1*

(Texas, Tennessee, California, Arizona, New Jersey, Georgia, and Virginia). Of the controlled property, six states (New Jersey, Texas, Tennessee, Georgia, Alabama, and Kentucky) receive over half. New Jersey alone receives approximately 17 percent of controlled property transfers, a point emphasized in Figure 3.2.

Losses, Suspensions, and Terminations

In FYs 2014 to 2016, LESO suspended 268 LEAs and terminated 24. Next, we analyze these suspensions and terminations, their justifications, and the LEAs involved.

Nearly all suspended LEAs were state LEAs. Of the 268 LEA suspensions, 267 were state LEAs, one tribal, and none federal. Of the suspensions at the state level, 259 unique LEAs were suspended. Figure 3.3 is a heat map of states by their total number of LEA suspensions. Notably, North Carolina had 23 percent of all LEA suspensions during this period, and Montana had 10 percent. Furthermore, the U.S. Virgin Islands and seven states (Alabama, Alaska, North Carolina, New Jersey, Minnesota, Ohio, and Rhode Island) were suspended during the period (above and beyond the individual LEAs suspended within those states).

Figure 3.2
Controlled Property Transfers by State, FY 2015–2017

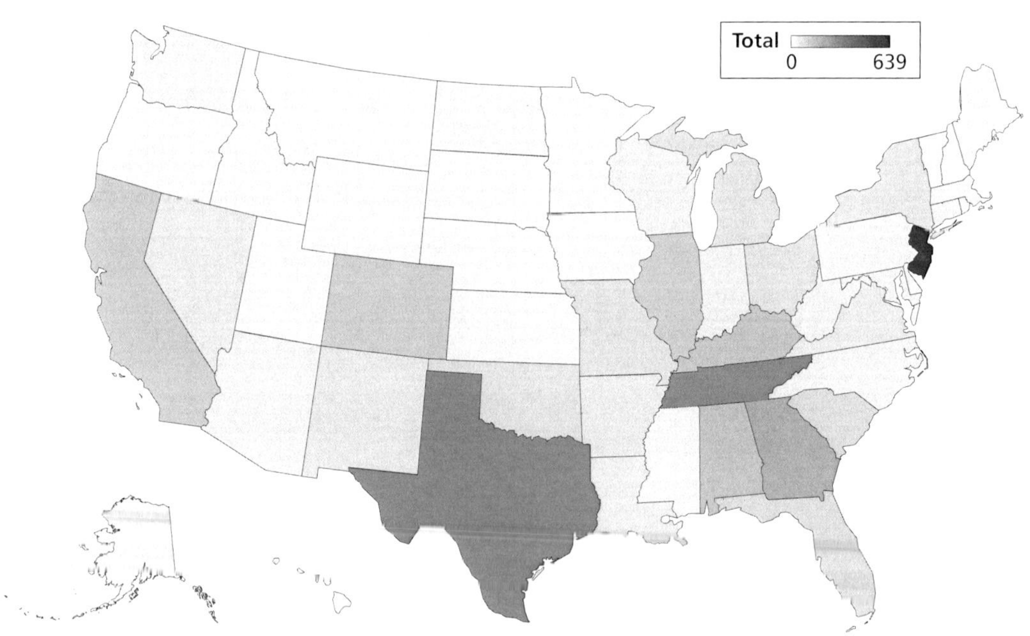

SOURCE: Data provided by LESO to RAND.
RAND *RR2464-3.2*

Figure 3.3
Map of Total LEA Suspensions by State, FY 2014–2016

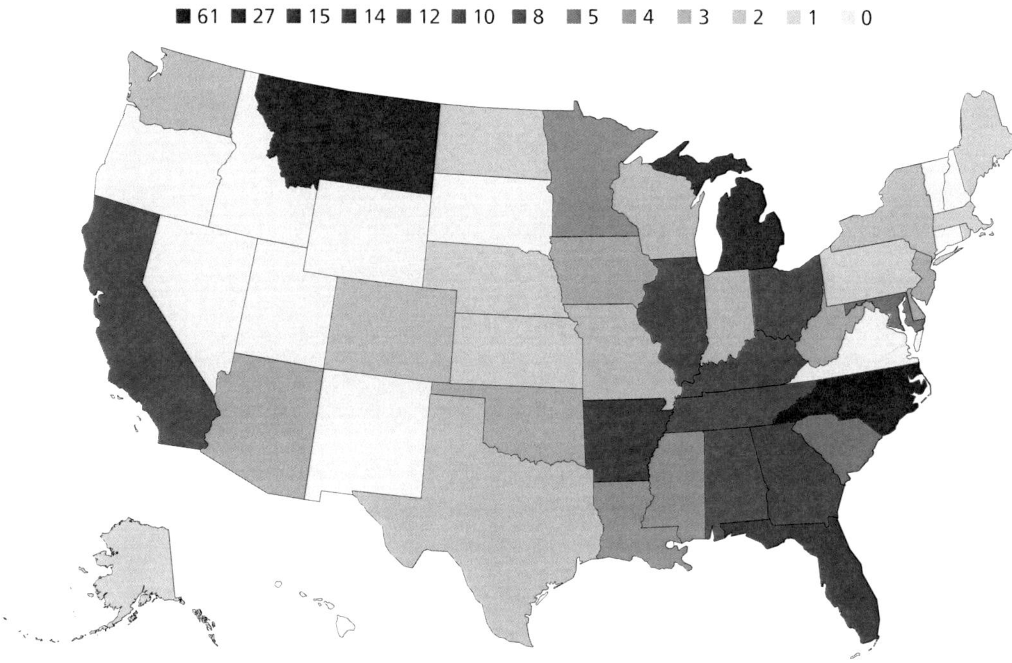

SOURCE: Data provided by LESO to RAND.
NOTE: Figure does not include the U.S. Virgin Islands, where there was one suspension.
RAND *RR2464-3.3*

There are several possible explanations for the different numbers of suspensions by state. We first considered the official justifications. Table 3.8 shows the justifications that the LESO office provided for the suspensions, along with the total times each justification was given. "Lost, missing, stolen, and damaged weapons" is the most frequent justification, while "state coordinator requests" for the suspensions (based on chronic violations of program requirements) is second.

During FYs 2014 to 2016, 24 LEAs were terminated. As shown in Table 3.9, more than half of the terminations occurred in North Carolina, a state that was suspended in its entirety while also having the majority of individual LEA suspensions.

As with suspensions, justifications were given for each of the 24 terminations (see Table 3.10). While LEA noncompliance with LESO controls was the major driver of the terminations, protracted issues with lost, missing, or stolen weapons was the second-most-frequent cause of the terminations. The majority of terminations (67 percent) were initiated by state coordinators.

Table 3.8
LESO Justification for Suspensions, FY 2014–2016

Justification	Total
Grand total	*268*
L/M/S/D weapon	115
State coordinator request	49
Program violation	39
MOA/application discrepancy	35
Misappropriation of property	13
No POC assigned	11
Other	3
MOA violation	2
Program compliance	1

SOURCE: Data provided by LESO to RAND.

NOTE: POC = point of contact.

Table 3.9
Total LEA Terminations by State, FY 2014–2016

State	Total	Percentage of Total
Grand total	*24*	*100%*
NC	14	58%
IL	2	8%
AR	1	4%
AZ	1	4%
GA	1	4%
KY	1	4%
MN	1	4%
MT	1	4%
TX	1	4%
WV	1	4%

SOURCE: Data provided by LESO to RAND.

NOTE: Percentages do not sum to 100 due to rounding.

Table 3.10
LESO Justification for Terminations, FY 2014–2016

Reason	Total
LEA not compliant	17
L/M/S weapon	4
Misappropriation of government property	1
Not eligible	1
LEA no longer in existence	1

SOURCE: Data provided by LESO to RAND.

Rebuys of Excess Equipment

In April 2016, Senator Claire McCaskill of Missouri expressed concern in a letter to the Principal Deputy Under Secretary of Defense for Acquisition, Technology and Logistics that DoD was declaring as excess a number of items that were new or in like-new condition and giving them away to state and local law enforcement and other federal agencies while purchasing new versions of those same items in the same year. In a response to the query, the Office of the Secretary of Defense provided data on equipment purchased and on serviceable equipment, or condition code "A" equipment, transferred under the LESO program between 2011 and 2015. The data were limited to the following types of controlled and prohibited equipment, accounting for a total transfer value of just $105 million over five years (in contrast with a value of more than $1.5 billion in all categories of controlled and prohibited equipment currently held by LEAs, as itemized in Table 3.1):[4]

1. firearms and firearm parts of all types, including rifles, pistols, shotguns, machine guns, and grenade launchers
2. trucks, watercraft, and aircraft of all types, including utility trucks, tractors, dump trucks, semitrailers, tanks, armored trucks, MRAPs, boats, airplanes, and helicopters
3. bayonets and knives
4. tasers
5. grenades, flash bang grenades, grenade launchers, and grenade launcher attachments
6. night-vision equipment, including goggles, viewers, viewing sets, scopes, sightings, sight assemblies, and image intensifiers

[4] In discussions with RAND researchers, DLA LESO personnel indicated they are unable to fully answer the Senator's question without purchase data from all the DoD services and other federal agencies that have received excess property, citing costs and effort because the data sets are enormous and not readily accessible.

7. camouflage equipment, including clothing, radar-scattering nets, and screening systems.[5]

To our knowledge, DoD did not analyze these data to determine how often and to what extent DoD bought new equipment at the same time it sent serviceable materiel to LEAs. We obtained the data provided to Senator McCaskill, which we regard as incomplete because a thorough analysis would require data on the redistribution of excess equipment to all customers, and not just to LEAs. However, the DoD response to Senator McCaskill did include over 1,800 pages of condition-A raw purchase and transfer data from 2011 to 2015, as well as an interpretation of the data sets. DoD concluded that less than 3 percent of reparable items that were turned in to DLA as excess had also been purchased within a year. Moreover, according to DLA LESO 2015 data, none of the top 25 most-expensive categories of items transferred to LEA had been repurchased in the same year. Nonetheless, after reviewing the five-year DoD data, which did not contain all of DoD's component purchasing data, we do not believe that the DoD response included an analysis of all such purchasing data. A more complete analysis, based on acquiring the data on all redistribution actions, could not be undertaken by us; such an analysis was beyond the scope of this project in terms of the time limitations, data processing capacity, and sponsor mandate. Determining the amount of equipment that is repurchased is not straightforward. For example, distribution of condition code A equipment to LEAs covers only part of the total volume of distribution, and a lot of the equipment goes to other DoD customers.

---

[5] Principal Deputy Under Secretary of Defense, Acquisition, Technology, and Logistics, "Oversight of Federal Programs for Equipping State and Local Law Enforcement," letter to U.S. Senator Claire McCaskill, January 19, 2017.

CHAPTER FOUR

Stakeholder Interviews

In this chapter, we describe our interviews with LESO program stakeholders. We conducted these interviews with LESO state coordinators and state points of contact (POCs), officials from LEAs who participate in the LESO program, and representatives of national organizations.

State Coordinators and State Points of Contact

We contacted representatives from states and territories that participate in the LESO program to gather their opinions of the program, as well as public perceptions. The sample, which included 20 states and two territories, is geographically diverse and representative of varying levels of program participation.

We developed a standardized interview guide (see Appendix C), which included questions about how the program is being implemented, what the individual LEA equipment holdings are, and the program benefits and challenges from the perspective of both the state coordinator and the LEAs. We contacted representatives from each state or territory and provided them with a letter of support from the LESO program office encouraging participation. All interviews were conducted on a nonattribution basis, with the understanding that results would be presented only in aggregate and that specific responses would not be attributed to individuals or to states or territories. Ultimately, a total of 11 representatives from nine states and two territories from the original sample were interviewed.

We conducted interviews in July, August, and September 2017, by phone or in person at the annual LESO State Coordinator Conference in Norfolk, Virginia. Although significant policy changes to the LESO program were announced by the White House near the end of this period, we used the same interview protocol for all interviews. We interviewed either the state coordinator, the state POC, or both.

In keeping with our promise to protect the privacy of the state representatives whom we interviewed, we summarize many of our findings from these interviews by referring below to "most," "many," "several," or "some" respondents who offered similar interview responses in particular cases. As one would expect, "most" refers to more than half of the total 11 respondents. "Many" refers to between a third and a half of the 11 respondents. "Several" refers to between a quarter and a third of the 11 respondents. And "some" refers to fewer than a quarter of the 11 respondents.

All respondents indicated that they had served in their current positions for at least a year and a half. Most told us there was a small number of personnel dedicated to the program and that those people worked either alone or with only one or two full- or part-time staff. Several indicated that the state coordinator position in their state was largely ceremonial and that the state POC handled all day-to-day operations. Although we did not ask respondents about their professional backgrounds, we learned, based on the information volunteered, that many respondents had prior law enforcement or military experience. Others had no experience in either field.

Respondents reported having as few as five and as many as 500 active LEAs in the program. Collectively, they reported acquiring the full range of controlled and uncontrolled equipment offered through the LESO program, ranging from office supplies to MRAPs to firearms.

We asked respondents whether they believed that equipment available through LESO was properly categorized as controlled, uncontrolled, or prohibited; what the impact of the 2015 EO had been on the program from their perspective; and how the process of acquiring EO-controlled equipment differed from the process for acquiring DoD-controlled equipment. Respondents told us that they generally believed that the categorization of equipment was appropriate, although if they did not, most often they told us that the categories were too restrictive. Several pointed out that many controlled items are readily available commercially and, therefore, require little or no justification if acquired through other means. The most frequently cited examples of items seen as being overclassified included heavy trucks and bayonets. Notably, however, respondents did not express a desire for easier access to weaponry or equipment that would be viewed as chiefly military; in this vein, several respondents suggested that even bayonets should be made available because they were not chiefly military but were simply utility knives and would be used as such.

Representatives from states and territories told us that the most significant change as a result of EO 13688 was the increase in the amount of paperwork and justification required to acquire certain types of equipment. Some indicated this was positive, as it reflected common sense ideas, increased accountability, and improved community buy-in. A slightly larger number indicated that the EO had caused some LEAs to drop out of the program or to stop requesting controlled items. Respondents reiterated that the primary difference between acquiring EO-controlled and DoD-controlled items was the additional paperwork and justifications required for EO-controlled items.

We asked the state and territorial representatives whether LEAs used equipment for counterdrug, counterterrorism, or border security; whether they encouraged LEAs to use these terms in their justifications; and how they believed LESO prioritized requests when these terms were used. Most respondents indicated that their jurisdictions used equipment at various times for all three purposes, with variations based on geography and background characteristics. The most commonly cited use was counterdrug operations, with border security cited least often. One respondent indicated that LEAs serving rural areas were more likely to request items for use in counterdrug operations, while LEAs in urban areas were more likely to request items for counterterrorism.

Some state coordinators told us that they encouraged LEAs to use keywords associated with counterdrug, counterterrorism, or border security operations in their justifications, while others did not because they wanted LEAs to provide their own justifications. Some reminded LEAs that these operations were emphasized by LESO. Among those respondents who encouraged LEAs to use the keywords, most advised LEAs to do so only if the equipment would be used for those purposes. They told us that they warned LEAs that they would look for evidence that items were being used for those purposes. Respondents generally indicated that they believed LESO prioritized distribution of items based on the keywords, although some noted that they did not believe LESO necessarily penalized requests that were not for these purposes. Another respondent indicated that LESO would send back requests for certain items that did not include a justification based on one of the three purposes.

We asked respondents about the items that were prohibited under EO 13688. Some indicated that they had returned prohibited items, while others have stored the items in a secure location, preventing further access or use by officers. These items often included bayonets, tracked vehicles, riot control gear, and rocket-propelled grenade launchers. Several respondents stressed that the names used by LESO for some items are misleading and do not reflect how items are actually used by law enforcement. For example, police weapons are not designed to accommodate the mounting of a bayonet, so LEAs use the bayonets as utility knives, not as weapons. Likewise, grenade launchers are not used by police for deploying grenades but for deploying nonlethal chemical irritants or smoke (tear gas canisters). We asked whether the result of these additional items being prohibited was that LEAs could not access them at all. Some respondents indicated that it was. In other cases, particularly when the items in question were bayonets, the respondents told us that they replaced them with similar knives, either bought commercially or, in one case, acquired through the LESO program. In still other cases, they told us that they acquired prohibited items using grant funds or by obtaining donations. One respondent reported having to return knee pads because of the camouflage pattern.

We asked respondents whether they thought that using controlled items increased the risk to officers or citizens. Most indicated that they thought the equipment reduced risk. They frequently cited the protective function of MRAPs, which allow officers to respond to a variety of dangerous situations. Others suggested that risk was more influenced by proper use and training than by the type of equipment. One respondent noted that because equivalents of the controlled items could be acquired commercially, their distribution through LESO did not alter risk because LEAs were already familiar with the equipment.

When asked whether they believed LEAs would have acquired equipment using their own budgets if that equipment had not been available through LESO, the responses of state coordinators varied. Many agreed that LEAs would not be able to afford higher-cost items and would buy only those items that were viewed as essential (e.g., medical kits and firearms). These characteristics applied regardless of whether the items in question were controlled or uncontrolled. We asked respondents how much it cost to participate in the program. In most cases, they told us that costs were under $200,000 and were limited to the salaries of the staff who administered the program, as well as the cost of shipping and making repairs so that the equipment is workable. Several state coordinators noted that they offset the costs of administering the program by charging either a flat annual fee per LEA or a fee based on a percentage of the acquisition cost of the items. Some respondents noted that costs were higher in years when they needed to travel to multiple LEAs to conduct verifications.

Respondents indicated that they checked whether LEAs already had the equipment they were requesting and would ask why more of the same item was necessary. Many noted that they looked at the written justifications for the request but did not pursue further information.

All respondents indicated that they took steps to ensure that equipment requested through the program would be used for law enforcement purposes. Some noted that they focused on communicating the program requirements to LEAs prior to requisition, while others told us they did site visits to verify that the equipment received through the program was being used for law enforcement.

We also asked respondents how they prioritized requests for equipment across the LEAs in their states and territories. Most indicated that they filled requests on a first come, first served basis, although several noted that they treated controlled property differently; for instance, they attempted to achieve an equitable distribution of items and prioritized if a particular item was scarce.

We asked respondents whether they ever rejected requests. Nearly all indicated that they did, citing a weak justification as the most frequent reason for rejection. Other reasons included LEAs already having the item requested, improper use, or a history of poor performance in the program. One respondent noted that good communication prevented rejections, while another described working with LEAs to adjust requests rather than rejecting them, particularly if the issue was that an LEA had requested too many of an item based on its number of sworn officers.

Most respondents indicated that LEAs sometimes sold uncontrolled equipment after ownership had been transferred to the LEAs, although three LEAs had rules specifically prohibiting such sales. Among those who reported that LEAs in their jurisdictions sold equipment after one year, several told us that they had rules in place requiring the proceeds to go to the LEA's law enforcement budget and not to the general-use funds. Some added that they took measures to ensure LEAs were not acquiring items to sell them later, including flagging repeated requests for the same item. One respondent indicated not knowing what LEAs did with uncontrolled items after a year had elapsed.

Five respondents indicated that their state or territory had been suspended from the program, with suspension lengths lasting from a few weeks to a year. Suspensions were the result of events attributable to the state or territory itself or to the LEA under the state's or territory's oversight. In all but one case, respondents agreed with the suspensions. In the other case, the respondent indicated that one suspension had been fair, but the second, which resulted from a stolen weapon, was unfair because the LEA had taken reasonable precautions. Several respondents indicated that the suspensions coincided with the LESO program's adoption of FEPMIS and that they were unable to comply with the new requirements. Other specific reasons for suspensions included being out of compliance with inventory or inspection rules, missing or stolen weapons, or not having the photos required to prove inspections had been conducted.

Among LEAs that had been suspended, respondents indicated that the LEAs took rectifying steps, from instituting new controls to completely reorganizing their programs. Several said that they now suspend LEAs when they believe an LEA is in danger of drifting off course. Two respondents indicated that they had added additional training for LEAs.

Respondents of states and territories that had been suspended noted that the suspensions did not change their relationships with LESO; most praised the office for its helpfulness and indicated that communication with LESO was excellent. Most also indicated that LESO does not need to make changes to help LEAs avoid being suspended. However, one respondent indicated that LESO did not document its rules adequately in writing, so LEAs were not always confident what behavior would result in a suspension.

We asked respondents how the controlled and uncontrolled equipment provided to LEAs through the LESO program helped LEAs with their law enforcement missions. Many noted that the cost savings achieved by receiving equipment through the LESO program allowed LEAs to do more than they would be able to do or to make purchases they could not otherwise have afforded. Most reported that the equipment improved officer safety, citing medical kits and MRAPs. Many said that equipment from LESO helped LEAs respond to natural disasters (e.g., using HMMVVs or MRAPs during hurricanes or being able to provide blankets and shelters). Some told us that vehicles obtained through the program were useful for traversing difficult terrain in remote areas and that they were being used either for search and rescue or on a daily basis, depending on the area. Several indicated, however, that it was beyond their expertise to assess whether LESO equipment helped LEAs in their crime-fighting mission; conversely, some noted that the equipment improved community relations by increasing LEA visibility and bolstered confidence in LEA capabilities.

We asked whether the state respondents considered public perceptions when deciding on equipment requests. Many indicated that they communicated with the requestor about potential criticism or local issues before submitting the request. Others told us that they did not and cited misperceptions about the program or about law enforcement in general. Several noted that the LESO program was often wrongly linked to events in Ferguson, Missouri, even though the equipment used there had not been obtained through the LESO program. We asked whether LEAs decided to obtain or use equipment differently as a result of public perceptions. Some told us they had always been careful, others stated that public perceptions did not influence their decisionmaking, and a few indicated they had become more selective. One interviewee noted that some LEAs had become wary of items with a military appearance, and others agreed that some LEAs either did not request certain items now or had decided to return some items.

Respondents indicated that, for controlled items, LEAs fulfilled the requirement for consent from the highest elected official in a variety of ways, depending on the underlying nature of the LEA and the local government. Police chiefs requested consent either from the mayor or from city or county council, as appropriate. Sheriffs, who are elected themselves, can provide their own consent but also need to show they had informed an elected civilian governing body. One respondent used a form created by another state to certify consent, while another noted that the state legislature had passed a bill requiring localities to indicate their consent for an LEA in their community to participate in the program and to acquire certain types of equipment.

When we asked how states and territories determined agency needs for LESO equipment, all respondents indicated that LEAs knew what they needed and that the state or territory reviewed the justification to make its determination.

Respondents indicated they were happy with the distribution of roles and oversight between LESO and other agencies and that they did not wish to see changes or a model that involved different agencies, such as DoJ. Many noted concerns about transportation costs, the speed of the acquisition process, and a lack of authority on the state coordinator's part to force LEAs to return equipment.

When asked whether there were downsides to receiving equipment through the program, respondents commented on its administrative burden. They also noted the lack of good information about equipment in the form of photos or accurate reports about its condition before the equipment was in hand. One respondent noted the negativity toward law enforcement using military equipment as a downside to participation. Despite these concerns, most respondents told us that the program was beneficial and that eligible entities should participate.

When asked whether they had received any complaints about LEA use of LESO equipment, respondents indicated that they had not received any *valid* complaints. Several noted that they received media inquiries, and two cited a ramp-up in concerns about the program as a result of political activity or upcoming elections.

Officials from Participating Law Enforcement Agencies

To decide which LEA officials to interview, we used data provided by LESO to determine which LEAs have the most equipment, in terms of both number and value for both controlled and uncontrolled equipment. We made four lists: most controlled items, most uncontrolled items, highest dollar value of controlled items, and highest dollar value of uncontrolled items. Our goal was to interview the top 25 LEAs on each of those lists. There was considerable overlap between these lists because the LEAs that had the most items also tended to have the most dollar value of items. As a result, we interviewed officials at fewer than 100 LEAs.

In honing the interview list, we reviewed a LESO-provided list of LEAs that were suspended from the program in FYs 2014 to 2016. Some were still suspended when we were planning our interviews, so we removed them to avoid potential lack of cooperation. We randomly selected several suspended but reinstated LEAs from our list to include in our sample.

Finally, we included LEAs in our list that have faced either recent perception issues or recent traumas, such as officer deaths in the line of duty. We felt agencies that had been publicly criticized for militarization or for threats to officer safety would add insight into the perceptions of the program. To determine which LEAs to include in this category, we reviewed literature and media from the past ten years, and we looked at the DoJ website for LEAs being investigated or under consent decree. We cross-checked the names of the LEAs found during this search with the LESO list of participating LEAs. If we found an LEA that was accused of militarization and had participated in the program, we added that LEA to the list. We focused on LEAs that had lost two or more officers in a single incident. We compiled that list, cross-checked it against the LESO list, and included a random selection of these LEAs in our sample.

In total, our sample included 79 LEAs from 27 states and two territories. As noted in the previous section, before we started the interviews, LESO sent out a letter of introduction to every state coordinator requesting cooperation in the evaluation. We contacted each state coordinator and asked for an introduction to the POC for each LEA in our sample. We also asked for the contact information for each LESO POC in each LEA so we could schedule interviews. Of the 29 states and territories we contacted, 23 responded and provided the LEA contact information and introductions. This narrowed our list of LEAs to 59. Our list was further narrowed to 47 when we dropped Texas and Florida because of hurricanes Harvey and Irma.

When we contacted each LEA, we reassured them that interviews were for nonattribution and that the findings would be reported only in aggregate. Of the 47 LEAs we contacted for an interview, 23 agreed to speak with us about the program, resulting in interviews of a total of 23 representatives from the 23 LEAs.

We used an interview protocol to guide our interviews (see Appendix D). We conducted the interviews by phone between August 14 and September 14, 2017. The interview protocol referenced program requirements under EO 13688. However, as noted elsewhere, President Trump issued EO 13809 revoking EO 13688 and rescinding any actions taken by LESO pursuant to EO 13688. As this happened in the middle of our analysis, we did not alter our protocol. Eighteen of the interviews we conducted occurred on the same day or after EO 13809 was issued.

Once again, in keeping with our promise to protect the privacy of the LEA officials whom we interviewed, we summarize many of our findings from these interviews by referring hereafter to "most," "many," "several," or "a few" respondents who offered similar interview responses in particular cases. As one would expect, "most" refers to more than half of the total 23 respondents. "Many" refers to between a third and a half of the 23 respondents. "Several" refers to between a quarter and a third of the 23 respondents. And "a few" refers to fewer than a quarter of the 23 respondents.

Respondents came from LEAs that varied in size, ranging from as few as six sworn officers to more than 10,000 officers. Length of participation in the program also varied. One LEA joined less than a year ago, and another had been affiliated since the program's inception. Furthermore, the jobs of the respondents varied; several worked in quartermaster units or support services units, and others served as patrol officers. In one case, the respondent was serving as the elected sheriff. Respondents who worked in specialized or emergency service units noted that participation in the LESO program was valuable because their LEA's focus was on acquiring specialized equipment (e.g., bomb detection robots or equipment for emergency services).

Most respondents reported that one or two people managed the LESO program in their LEA, although this varied by LEA size. One large LEA had four full-time personnel dedicated to the LESO program. Several respondents reported spending as little as one hour per week on the program, although others reported spending more time, with the most common response being a few hours a day or a few hours a week. At the high end, one LEA reported spending at least 40 hours per week administering the program. Respondents noted that the time they spent on the program varied with the level of activity.

Respondents had acquired the full range of equipment from LESO, including weapons (e.g., long guns), Humvees, MRAPs and other vehicles, and aircraft, as well as uncontrolled items, including duffel bags, first aid kits, tourniquets, and tool kits. One smaller LEA reported that it shared an MRAP acquired through the LESO program with neighboring LEAs.

Many officials indicated that equipment was properly categorized as controlled or uncontrolled. One interviewee told us that the categorization of controlled items was "clear and obvious." Several suggested that they believed the categorization was appropriate, but they cited one or two exceptions, which they seemed to regard as minor. Items such as axes, cold weather gear, knee pads, and optics for weapons were cited as examples of items categorized as controlled that should not be. A few noted that some characteristics of an item, such as armor, made it controlled, while similar equipment without that feature was not. Riot shields were the item most frequently cited as being improperly categorized as a controlled item. One respondent told us about an item acquired through LESO that was controlled when acquired, but not when another LEA in the same state acquired the same item. The respondent suspected this was due to an administrative or coding error. A small number of LEAs were critical of the way items were categorized.

Most officials reported using controlled equipment for counterdrug, counterterrorism, or border security. Counterdrug and counterterrorism uses were more frequently reported than were border security uses, although this is likely a factor of geography. Frequently reported uses included serving high-risk warrants and event or facility security. Equipment used for these purposes included helicopters, long guns, and such vehicles as MRAPs and Humvees. Several respondents told us they used equipment acquired through LESO to respond to natural disasters, with uses including cold weather protection and high-water rescue. Such specialized vehicles as MRAPs and Humvees were frequently cited in these examples.

Several respondents indicated that while they used equipment acquired from LESO for counterdrug, counterterrorism, or border security, they did not use these terms as keywords in their justifications to request the equipment. Many told us that they did not know how LESO used the keywords in prioritizing equipment distribution. Most thought that the program was first come, first served. One noted that most police work has some nexus to counterdrug or counterterror operations. Others told us that they believed the use of keywords was how LESO prioritized equipment, with one LEA official noting that they were "magic words."

Most respondents had not had to return equipment because it had become prohibited under EO 13688. Of those that did, the most common items returned or destroyed were bayonets, riot shields, and tracked vehicles.

Most interviewees told us that the EO had not changed whether they were able to acquire controlled or prohibited equipment. Some reported buying items such as ballistic helmets and vests, as well as riot control gear, using other funding sources. LEAs that had returned tracked vehicles indicated that they did without them or, in one case, replaced a tracked vehicle with a different, nontracked vehicle. Smaller LEAs were more likely to report going without items, while larger LEAs were more likely to acquire the items through alternate sources.

A small number of LEAs noted that the EO halted their acquisition of controlled equipment from LESO. The reasons included not wanting to acquire items they depended on but might have to give back (e.g., rifles) or items they needed to repair but might have to give back. Some told us that the program had become too onerous or had invited too much scrutiny from the media and other groups. The issue of public perception came up several times.

We asked the officials whether they would have acquired the equipment they received through LESO by other means if the program did not exist, what impact the LESO program had on their budgets, and whether they had sold items acquired through the program.

Officials at larger LEAs indicated that they would still have obtained most of the controlled and uncontrolled items through other sources, such as grants, although two such officials noted that they would not have an aviation program if not for aircraft acquired through LESO. Most noted savings to their budgets from participating in the program, often citing figures in the millions. Among the larger LEAs, most officials said they had not sold items acquired through the program, although one indicated transferring items to other LEAs and another mentioned selling a truck acquired through the program. (The truck was no longer needed and had been sold for a fraction of the cost the LEA had paid to requisition and transfer the vehicle.) Other than the noted impact on aviation, officials at larger departments did not express concerns about major impacts if the departments could not obtain controlled equipment from LESO.

Among smaller LEAs, many noted that they used the program specifically to acquire items they could not otherwise afford. Some indicated that they would have acquired the equipment anyway but that being able to do so for lower cost allowed them to use the savings on other items they would not otherwise have been able to afford. Officials at a few of the smaller LEAs did note, however, that they would have gone without LESO items because they were not essential; these were typically uncontrolled items. MRAPs, aircraft, and rifles were among the controlled items most frequently cited by LEAs as ones they would have been unlikely to acquire if the LESO program did not exist. One respondent noted that the cost of an MRAP would have exceeded the LEA's entire annual budget.

Officials at many smaller LEAs noted that not being able to obtain controlled equipment through the LESO program would have had major impacts on them, because this was the only way they could acquire such equipment. The cited impacts included reductions in officer safety and in LEA emergency preparedness and readiness.

Like officials at larger LEAs, officials at smaller LEAs did not typically report selling equipment they had acquired through the LESO program. Some noted they were not permitted to do so, although it was unclear whether they were referring to LESO rules or to their LEA's or state's policies. Others noted that they did not sell equipment but that they transferred it to other LEAs and received transfer items in return. One LEA cited an instance where equipment had been sold under a prior presidential administration.

As noted previously, we included LEAs that had been suspended from the LESO program but reinstated. Among LEAs that indicated they had been suspended, the most common reason was lost weapons. Other reasons included improper destruction of equipment and being late with an inventory report. Two LEAs reported cases of fraud or misuse of equipment outside the LEA by a prior agency administration. Reported suspension lengths ranged from 60 days to a year. While most officials indicated that they agreed with the suspensions, one noted that an LEA had taken reasonable measures to secure a weapon that had been stolen and believed the suspension to be too harsh. Another indicated that while the suspension was merited, the length of the suspension had been excessive.

Most who had been suspended indicated that they had made changes as a result, generally focusing on improved accountability and documentation, and that their interactions with the LESO program and their state coordinator had improved. Some indicated they had not made any changes because they were already taking appropriate measures.

When we asked what LESO could change to help prevent LEAs from being suspended, standardizing and clarifying rules was the most frequent answer. Ensuring that state coordinators enforced rules was the second–most common answer. Some indicated that no changes were needed, but several indicted that, while they were appreciative of their state coordinators, they believed LESO was not sufficiently responsive or proactive in providing written policies and rules.

We asked LEA officials to describe how equipment acquired through the LESO program helped in their law enforcement missions. Officials told us they used equipment for hostage and other high-threat situations, for periods of heightened security, and for natural disaster response (e.g., flood operations/rescues, ice storms, and access to remote areas). Some noted they had used medical equipment acquired from LESO to save lives. MRAPs, IED detection robots, and aircraft were among the items most commonly cited for officer safety and crime prevention missions.

We asked respondents how they addressed the requirement to obtain consent from the highest elected official for requests for controlled equipment. Responses were consistent with program rules: Respondents in cities with mayors indicated they worked with the mayor's office, which sometimes resulted in delays. One respondent's LEA had drafted a resolution, which was approved by the county legislature. The resolution allowed the LEA to acquire certain types of items; a new resolution would be required if the LEA decided to acquire other items not covered in the current resolution. Respondents in jurisdictions with sheriff's departments reported that the sheriffs approve requests for controlled items.

We asked respondents whether they considered public perceptions when deciding whether to request controlled equipment. Many noted that their elected leaders now provide guidance about obtaining and using controlled equipment. Some noted that they no longer acquire controlled equipment due to public perceptions. Others noted that they focus on education, working with the media, elected officials, and the community to improve understanding. One respondent noted that minor actions, such as painting a LESO-provided vehicle (e.g., an MRAP), made a huge difference in community perceptions. Two respondents noted that controlled equipment had a positive impact, with items like MRAPs drawing attention from children and others when they were displayed at public events.

Most noted that their LEA's position on whether to obtain and how to use certain types of equipment had not changed due to public perceptions. Many indicated that this was the case because they had always been careful about community relations and had acquired items only if needed. However, some reported that they considered equipment more carefully or involved elected leaders in decisions. One respondent noted that they now avoid items with a military appearance, and, as noted earlier, some told us that they no longer acquire controlled equipment.

Most officials did not recommend changes in the roles played by LESO or their state coordinators. Several praised their state coordinators. Respondents were more likely to be critical of LESO than of state coordinators, citing DLA policy or generally the administrative burdens placed upon those who manage the program. Reasons for the criticisms included the lack of standardization and clarity regarding rules. A few noted that some LESO rules made no sense. One respondent told us that, under program rules, a glow stick could be acquired and used for marking a road in an emergency—but if that same glow stick were given to a child at a community event, the LEA would be suspended from the program for using it for a non–law enforcement purpose.

Most respondents did not see any downside to participating in the program. Those who did cited issues with the functionality of the website or problems that resulted from inaccurate or incomplete information about items. One interviewee told us that "some junk gets through the system" and gets delivered to LEAs as a result. The administrative burden was also cited, although some LEAs noted it was appropriate for items of this nature. One respondent cited operational concerns resulting from needing to pull weapons from officers on the street to conduct the LESO-required inventory.

Finally, we asked LEA officials to estimate what they had saved as a result of participating in the program. Responses ranged from the hundreds of thousands to millions of dollars. We also asked what it cost to participate in the program. Here, costs were often identified as in-kind costs in labor hours spent by LEA staff on the program; some reported costs in the thousands, and a few noted costs in the hundreds of thousands. The cited costs often included transportation for the acquired equipment. Although we did not do a cost/benefit analysis, the savings reported by LEA officials from participation exceeded the costs they reported—often by several orders of magnitude. In Table 4.1, we summarize the results.[1]

---

1 There are costs or user fees imposed upon some LEAs depending upon the individual state's program management policy. The fees help pay for the program overhead. DLA LESO requires that LEAs assume the transportation costs associated with shipping items or self-service pick up at one of the distribution points located throughout the country and do not impose any other user fees.

Table 4.1
Costs and Benefits of LESO Program Among Surveyed LEAs

	Minimum ($)	Maximum ($)
Estimated program savings/year	100,000	15,000,000
Estimated participation cost/year	700	600,000
Estimated cost of maintaining program/year	175	100,000

SOURCE: RAND structured discussions and interviews with LEA representatives.

Representatives from National Organizations

Numerous groups outside Congress and the LESO program have a stake in and an opinion about the program. These include the NAACP, Police Foundation, ACLU, International Association of Campus Law Enforcement Administrators (IACLEA), Fraternal Order of Police (FOP), and the National Organization of Black Law Enforcement Executives (NOBLE). From our interviews, as well as comments in the public record, most of the stakeholders' positions can be summarized as generally supportive of the LESO program but with suggestions for how to improve it.

The NAACP, for example, is concerned with some equipment, such as assault rifles, MRAPs, and bayonets. This concern stems from the perception that LEAs use what they get even if it does not make sense. NAACP leaders expressed support for policies to govern how and when to use certain types of equipment. For bayonets, for example, they noted that while they could be used to cut seatbelts, other tools designed for this task would not risk collateral damage.

Leaders from the Police Foundation addressed the issue of additional oversight. They recommended that DoJ provide general guidance and that Congress be more prescriptive about the use and oversight of the program. Police Foundation leaders did not think LESO should decide how LEAs use equipment but did think LESO should set guidelines. Law enforcement experts should provide the guidance on equipment use, according to these leaders.

IACLEA administrators reported that the LESO program helps their mission, but they were concerned about the perceptions that the public might have of some of the equipment. They argued that DoJ and DHS should assume an advisory role, not a directive one, and that the state coordinators should be public safety officials, not politicians or police officers. These administrators believe that controls on certain equipment are appropriate because using some types of controlled equipment can increase risk to the community.

NOBLE advocates community awareness and responsible use of excess military equipment. Leaders of NOBLE are satisfied with the current categories of controlled equipment but argue that there should be ongoing review and routine consultation with the LESO program's governing body. They suggest that DoJ and DHS, along with DoD, should have oversight of the program. They also believe that the community lacks knowledge of the equipment involved and that greater transparency is needed.

CHAPTER FIVE

Public Perceptions

In this chapter, we describe the results from RAND's survey of public perceptions. The American public is a key stakeholder in the LESO program, its use of tax dollars, and its impact on policing. However, the view of the American public on the value of the program has been understudied. Using the RAND American Life Panel, a nationally representative, probability-based panel of U.S. citizens over the age of 18, we surveyed 1,044 people to gain an understanding of the perspective of the broader public.[1] Although many Americans are unaware of the program, the idea of the program has the support of the majority, albeit with restrictions.

We asked participants the following questions:

1. Overall, how satisfied are you with the quality of police services in your neighborhood?
2. Do you perceive your local police/law enforcement agency to be adequately equipped?
3. Are you aware of federal programs that provide excess military equipment to police/law enforcement agencies?
4. Excess military equipment includes everything from desks and first-aid kits to guns, vehicles, and aircraft. Equipment not transferred to police may be otherwise sold to the public or destroyed. Assume there is adequate local civilian oversight of the request. Should the types of equipment transferred be limited even if it means the equipment might be destroyed?

As depicted in Figure 5.1, 82 percent of respondents are either satisfied or very satisfied with police services in their neighborhoods. A small percentage (6 percent) is very dissatisfied.

When asked whether their local LEAs are adequately equipped, 63 percent of respondents said they are, 16 percent responded that they are underequipped, and 4 percent said they are overequipped. Results are shown in Figure 5.2.

[1] Michael Pollard and Matthew D. Baird, *The RAND American Life Panel: Technical Description*, Santa Monica, Calif.: RAND Corporation, RR-1651, 2017.

Figure 5.1
Overall, How Satisfied Are You with the Quality of Police Services in Your Neighborhood?

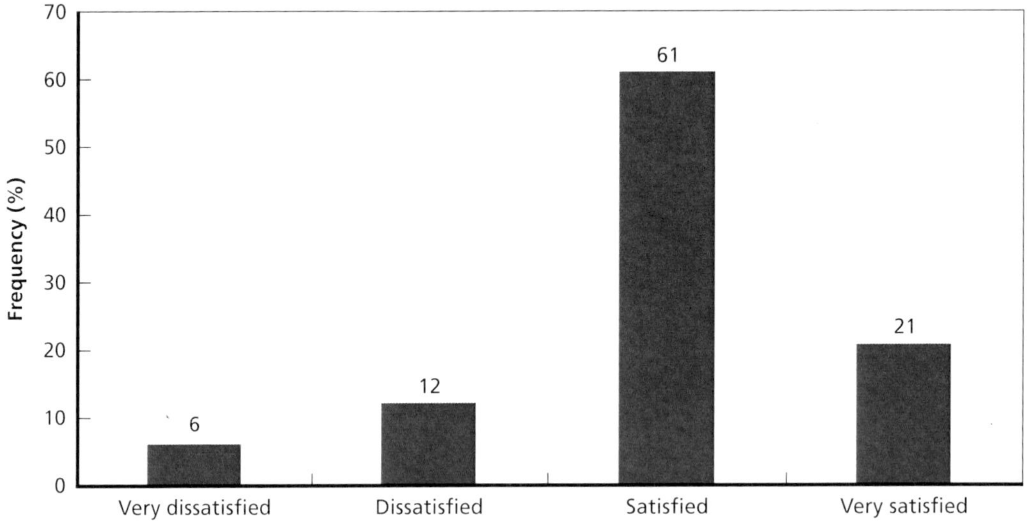

SOURCE: RAND American Life Panel.
RAND *RR2464-5.1*

Figure 5.2
Do You Perceive Your Local Police/Law Enforcement Agency to Be Adequately Equipped?

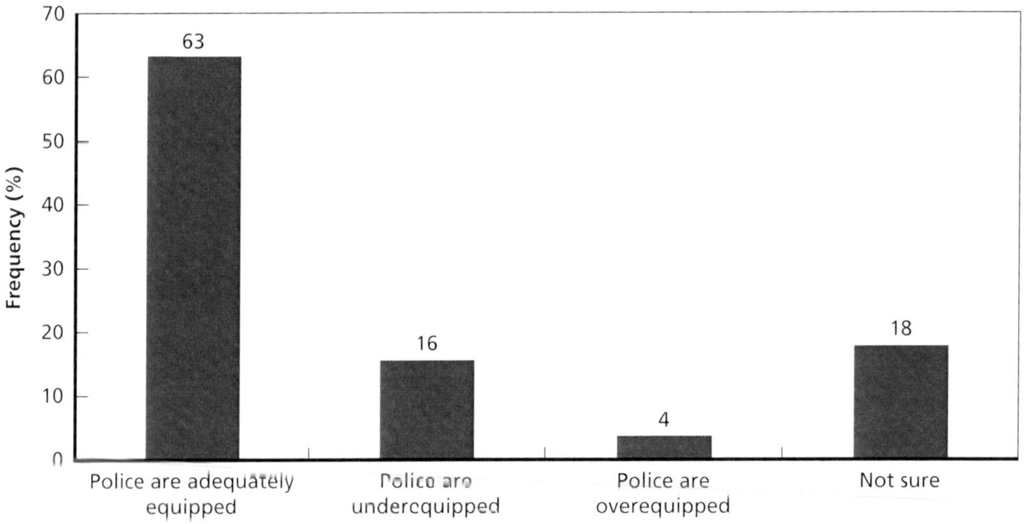

SOURCE: RAND American Life Panel.
RAND *RR2464-5.2*

When asked about federal programs that provide LEAs with excess military equipment, 48 percent of participants were unaware such programs existed, 33 percent find military transfers valuable, and 20 percent find them detrimental. However, as shown in Figure 5.3, differentiating by occupation makes a difference. Respondents working in the protective services[2] are significantly more likely to be aware of these programs and to find them valuable to the community.[3] Interestingly, the percentage of respondents working in protective services that view these programs as detrimental to the community is nearly the same as for all other respondents (21 percent and 20 percent, respectively). However, the large percentage of the population (48 percent) that is unaware of the program highlights the need for more education and greater transparency.

Responses to our fourth question revealed that many prefer restrictions on the program. As shown in Figure 5.4, 46 percent of respondents support limiting the program (41 percent to nonlethal equipment and 5 percent to no equipment at all),

Figure 5.3
Are You Aware of Federal Programs That Provide Excess Military Equipment to Police/Law Enforcement Agencies?

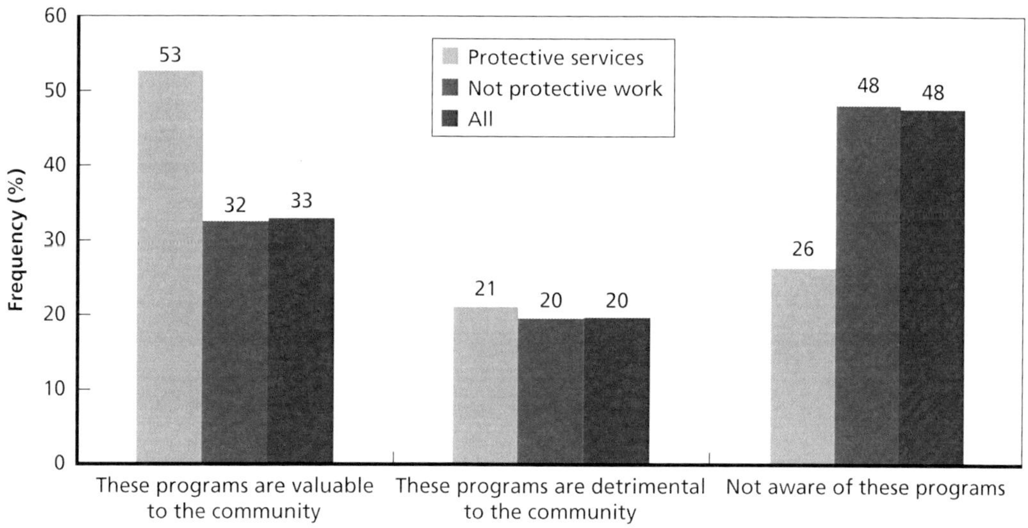

SOURCE: RAND American Life Panel.
RAND *RR2464-5.3*

---

[2] Police officers and criminal investigators; fish and game wardens; parking enforcement workers; police and sheriff's patrol officers; transit and railroad police; animal control workers; private detectives and investigators; security guards and gaming surveillance officers; crossing guards; transportation security screeners; lifeguards and other recreational workers, and all other protective service workers.

[3] The difference between respondents working in the protective services and others is highly statistically significant (t-stat = –69.699, *p*-value < 2.2E–16). In fact, the differences between the two groups are statistically significant for all questions asked.

Figure 5.4
Should Types of Equipment Transferred to LEAs Be Limited?

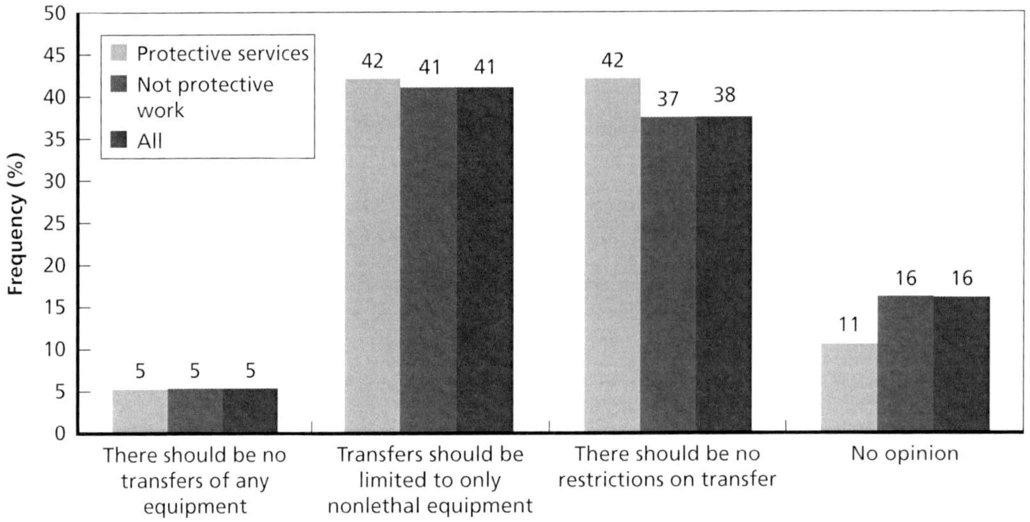

SOURCE: RAND American Life Panel.
RAND *RR2464-5.4*

while 38 percent do not think there should be limits and the other 16 percent had no opinion.[4]

Public opinion on military transfers is influenced by demographics. As shown in Figure 5.5, older respondents are more likely both to know of the LESO program and to support it.[5] Additionally, as shown in Figure 5.6, program support is significantly lower among black and Hispanic[6] respondents, who are also less likely to know of the program than are white respondents.[7]

Delving more into the age breakdown, more respondents over 70 support the program without restrictions than prefer restrictions. (Forty-eight percent of those over 70 prefer no restrictions, while 41 percent support the program limited to nonlethal equipment, and 4 percent do not support any equipment transfers.)[8] For all other age groups, fewer support the program without restrictions than support restricting the

---

[4] Figure 5.4 displays a statistically significant (t = –84.874, *p*-value < 2.2e–16) difference between respondents working in the protective services.

[5] The difference between the youngest (21–34) and oldest (70 and above) respondents is statistically significant at the 99-percent confidence level (t-stat = 3.6, *p*-value = 0.0004).

[6] Note that we restrict Hispanic to nonwhite and nonblack respondents.

[7] The differences between white and black (t-stat = –4.41, *p*-value = 2.16E-5) and white and Hispanic (t-stat = –4.52, *p*-value = 1.5E-5) groups are statistically significant at the 99-percent confidence level. The difference between black and Hispanic (t-stat = -0.24, *p*-value = 0.81) groups is not significant.

[8] The differences between respondents by age are not statistically significant.

Figure 5.5
Program Support Responses by Respondent Age

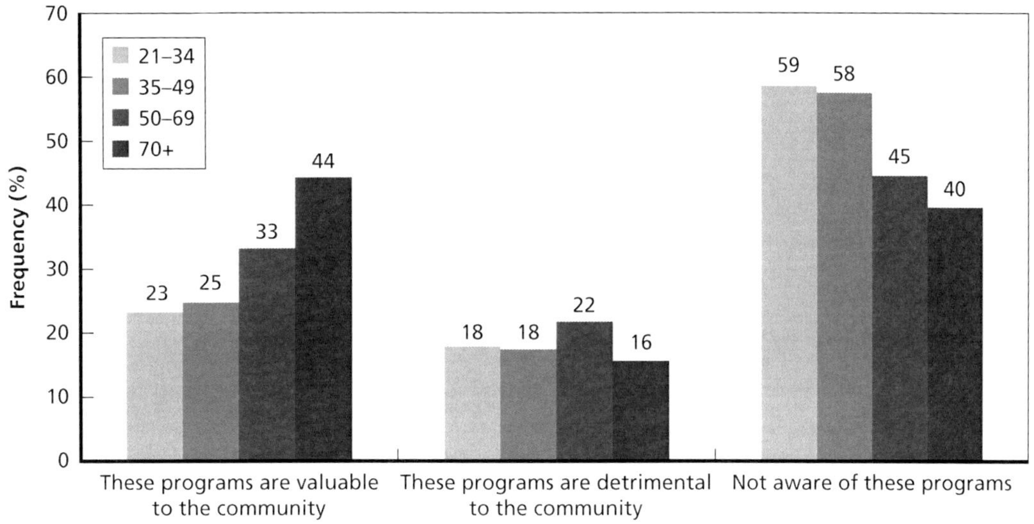

SOURCE: RAND American Life Panel.
RAND *RR2464-5.5*

Figure 5.6
Program Support Responses by Respondent Race

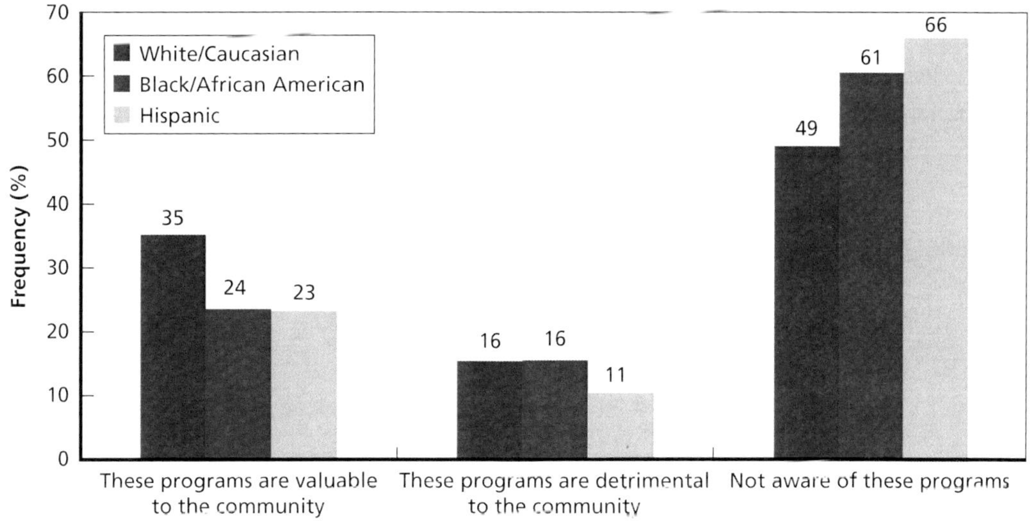

SOURCE: RAND American Life Panel.
RAND *RR2464-5.6*

program to either nonlethal equipment or no equipment at all. This is especially apparent for the youngest participants, of whom 55 percent support restrictions (50 percent limited to nonlethal and 5 percent to no transfers at all) and only 26 percent support the program without restrictions. These results are shown in Figure 5.7.

Transferring equipment to LEAs also has stronger support among white respondents than it does among black and Hispanic respondents. The results in Figure 5.8 reveal that when it comes to transfers without restrictions, 41 percent of white respondents support the idea, while only 23 percent of black and 22 percent of Hispanic respondents do. Similarly, 9 percent of Hispanic respondents and 8 percent of black respondents do not support any transfers of military equipment to LEAs, in comparison with 4 percent of white respondents.[9]

Results from the survey, weighted to be representative of the United States and current demographics, reveal a broad level of public support for local law enforcement, its equipment, and the use of the LESO program. However, the survey also points to areas of change. While the majority find the LESO program valuable to the community, the majority also believe in restricting the program in some way (41 percent believe there should be no transfers of lethal equipment). Results also reveal that a large share of the population is unaware of the LESO program's existence, pointing

Figure 5.7
Program Restriction Responses by Respondent Age

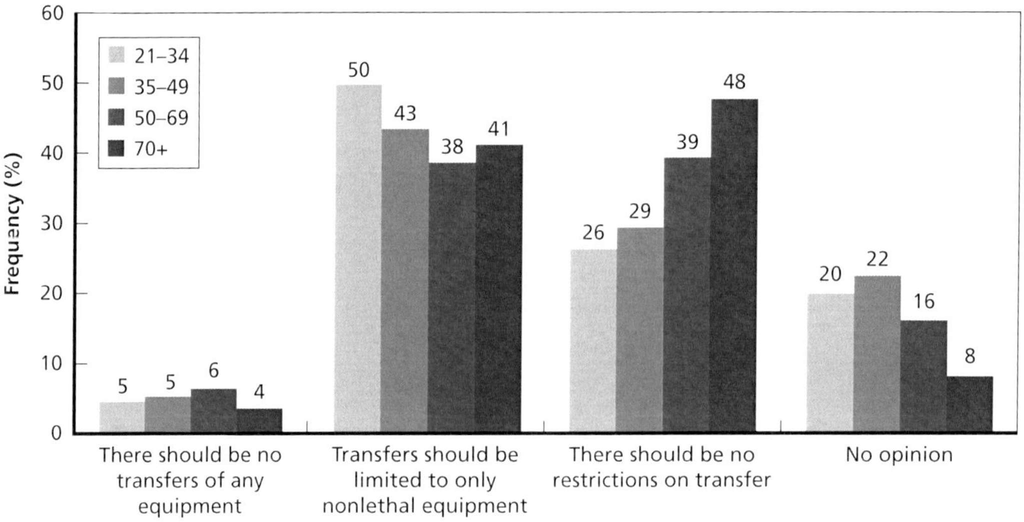

SOURCE: RAND American Life Panel.
RAND RR2464-5.7

[9] The differences between white and Hispanic (t-stat = 1.69, p-value = 0.09) groups are statistically significant at the 90-percent confidence level, while the differences between white and black (t-stat = 0.04, p-value = 0.97) and black and Hispanic (t-stat = 1.19, p-value = 0.23) are not significant.

Figure 5.8
Program Restriction Responses by Respondent Race

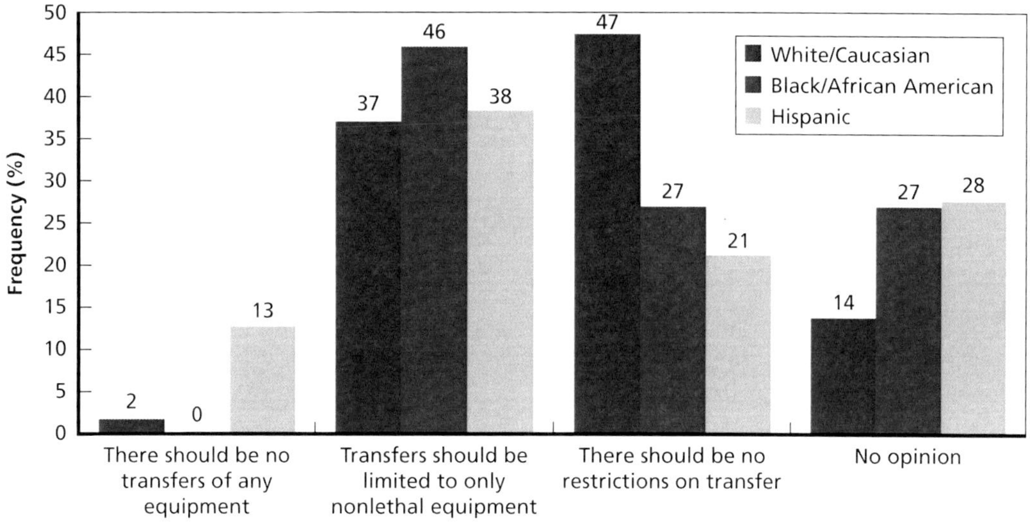

SOURCE: RAND American Life Panel.
RAND *RR2464-5.8*

to a potential lack in perceptions of transparency. These challenges are stronger for younger and minority groups, in which more lack program knowledge and those who find it less valuable believe more strongly in program restrictions. The RAND survey, thus, reveals that restrictions on transfers and efforts for community engagement, particularly with young and minority groups, could improve public support of the LESO program.

In sum, the survey of public perceptions highlighted that many Americans are unaware of the LESO program, indicating that additional public education and community outreach may increase public awareness. However, the idea of the program has the support of the majority, albeit with some restrictions. The bullets following summarize our key findings:

- Almost half of respondents (48 percent) report being unaware of programs that provide LEAs with excess military equipment, while 33 percent find military transfers valuable, and 20 percent find them detrimental.
- 46 percent of participants support limiting the program (41 percent to nonlethal equipment and 5 percent to no equipment at all), while 38 percent do not think there should be any limitations, and the other 16 percent had no opinion.
- Program support is significantly lower among black and Hispanic participants, who are also less likely to know of the program than are white participants.

CHAPTER SIX

Optional Paths Ahead

Throughout this evaluation, DLA leadership has been transparent, receptive to feedback, and eager to improve the program. Staff and officials are aware of their sensitive mission and the political and cultural issues surrounding it. We find that DLA has responded diligently to oversight and that the evolution of the program reflects that. With each incarnation, stronger and better controls have been put in place. However, the recurring GAO audits continue to stoke concerns about the effectiveness of program controls and the program's susceptibility to fraud.

Our analysis leaves one critical question unanswered: How can LESO, DLA, and, indeed, the U.S. government solve the "perception" problem? Despite evidence of an effective and efficiently managed program (at least as far as our research and limited data can indicate), the problems of perception—of police militarization and LESO's role in it—are likely to remain for the foreseeable future. Within this context, what options does the program have going forward?

In this chapter, we describe three potential paths ahead.

Maintain the Status Quo

The first, perhaps obvious, option is to leave the program as is. At least based on the assessment we were able to conduct, with the limited data that are currently available, there is no gross evidence of systemic failure. Indeed, we find that the LESO program is professionally managed, with some recurring issues but, overall, appropriate attention to managing to congressional intent. The program is popular with LEAs, even if there are minor complaints about bureaucracy and some elements of program administration. We find little evidence that DoD routinely disposes of and then repurchases excess equipment. However, to provide a more conclusive assessment of DoD purchases would require additional research and analysis of all DoD component purchase data, which is beyond the scope of this evaluation. Likewise, DLA has a fairly good record of keeping track of controlled equipment. And the vast majority of transfers—measured in quantities—are of general office equipment and other noncontroversial materials. Participating LEAs from smaller municipalities have also indicated that the controlled equipment offered through the LESO program enables and enhances their ability to more effectively perform missions with more–technologically advanced equipment, citing robots, thermal imaging, low-light optical equipment, and vehicles as game-changing technologies that offer officers a greater level of protection for higher-risk operations, to include "active shooter" and potential hostage situations.

Nonetheless, there are some issues with the status quo. These include modest program management issues, including whether there is a need to delineate qualifications for state coordinators, whether the training plans submitted by LEAs with equipment requests are effective, whether establishing additional fraud prevention measures would be beneficial, and whether local oversight and justification processes are thorough. In addition, there are no conclusive assessments of whether the focus on drug, border, and terrorism missions is distorting requests and otherwise diluting an understanding of the real reasons why jurisdictions are requesting equipment. Moreover, it is unclear whether those areas of emphasis are pushing law enforcement to focus on missions that they might not otherwise value so highly and, in so doing, aggravating relations with the community.

Keeping the program as is and addressing the areas highlighted could make the program more effective, but it would still not address the critical issue of police militarization.

Modify Program Emphasis and Distribution of Controlled Equipment

A second option is to keep the program largely as it is, but with some adjustments. Multiple modifications could be made, but two stand out as having the potential to change perceptions without fundamentally changing the character of the program.

The first modification would be to eliminate the preferential justifications for border, counterdrug, and counterterrorism missions. The counterdrug mission routinely brings police into contact with the citizenry, from activities as varied as routine patrol of drug markets to serving of warrants. While some in a neighborhood will appreciate a police presence to enforce drug laws, drug law enforcement is also a stressor in police-community relations.[1] As was reported in our interviews, the use of armored personnel carriers in serving high-risk drug warrants is likely to aggravate police-citizen tensions. In contrast, other uses of military-looking equipment, such as search and rescue, would be seen as more benign by community members and potentially gain wider acceptance as legitimate and more responsible uses of excess military equipment that is repurposed for civilian law enforcement activities.

[1] Greg Ridgeway, Terry L. Schell, Brian Gifford, Jessica Saunders, Susan Turner, Kevin Jack Riley, and Travis L. Dixon, *Police-Community Relations in Cincinnati*, Santa Monica, Calif.: RAND Corporation, MG-853-CC, 2009.

At this point, we do not know whether the preferential allocation of equipment to support these missions is driving LEAs to focus more on these missions than they otherwise would. If the allocation preferences are removed, over time we might observe a migration of requests toward less sensitive uses, such as humanitarian assistance or disaster response. Our interviews revealed inconsistent LEA use and state coordinator application of preferential justifications. The LEA interviews also revealed that the majority of transferred equipment is not directly used for policing but provides general consumables, first-responder and emergency response equipment that enhances officer safety in nonroutine operations, and some welcome budget relief to the smaller LEAs that have austere operating budgets.

A second modification would be to ensure that LESO is not the first provider of controlled equipment. Under such a scheme, an LEA requesting an MRAP or other potentially contentious equipment would have to first procure—perhaps even purchase—one from another source. The logic behind such a requirement is that the initial procurement of specialized equipment would provide a clearer signal to LESO, which has minimal expertise in law enforcement, about the priorities and capabilities of the LEAs requesting equipment. If an LEA already owned a piece of equipment that it was requesting from LESO, LESO would be able to determine the following:

- how the equipment is already integrated into operations and whether it has support from local officials
- whether the LEA has been able to maintain and operate the equipment it already has
- whether there are already personnel trained on the equipment.

This modification would come with some concerns. It could disadvantage smaller jurisdictions that might not have the "seed money" for an initial purchase or that might not need multiple pieces of the same equipment. Regardless, such a change in policy could relieve both DoD from the perception of militarizing police and DLA LESO from making law enforcement value judgments on the appropriate use of excess military property by LEAs.

Shift Responsibility for Controlled Equipment to Another Organization

A final option for the program is to move responsibility for decisions about the distribution and oversight of controlled equipment to another organization. There seems little need to move responsibility for the uncontrolled equipment, such as desks and office equipment, out of DLA. However, there is reasonable justification for moving responsibility for the controlled equipment, most probably to DoJ. Under this approach, DLA could maintain responsibility for its 42-day disposition time line, while responsibility for adjudicating individual controlled equipment requests would shift to DoJ. DoJ would, in turn, inform DLA about specific requests for controlled equipment.

At first glance, this approach might seem to introduce an additional step without commensurate benefit. However, there would likely be a number of advantages.

First, DoJ already has granting and programmatic relationships with most LEAs through programs administered by the Bureau of Justice Assistance (BJA) and, to a lesser extent, the National Institute of Justice (NIJ). This means there are accountability and monitoring systems already in place. BJA, NIJ, and other components in DoJ also help LEAs set and implement standards for new and emerging technologies, such as body armor, stun guns, and trigger locks. Simply put, these DoJ components are already closer than is DLA to the debate about whether LEAs should be encouraged to use certain types of equipment.

Second, DLA is ill-positioned to assess the value to law enforcement of excess DoD equipment in special emphasis areas such as counternarcotics, border control, and counterterrorism. DLA is similarly ill-equipped to answer—or even ask—questions about the impact that such transfers might have on police institutions. Do these emphases encourage police behaviors that exacerbate police-community tensions, as some have suggested? DoJ is better-positioned, through its existing evaluation programs and relations with LEAs, to provide answers to these questions.

Third, DLA and DoD more broadly have always been careful to ensure they do not get involved in domestic law enforcement activities. But this distance, while appropriate, is also awkward when it comes to ensuring the validity of state requests, certifying the development of state training plans, and interacting with state coordinators. While the current LESO program does not involve DLA in law enforcement activities, it necessarily does ask DLA to pass judgment on the soundness and suitability of law enforcement plans.

Fourth, lodging most program responsibility in DoJ could lead to the development of more insight into the effectiveness and consequences of equipment transfers. Potential advances unlikely to materialize under DLA management include both the development of standards for *monitoring* the use and employment of controlled equipment and the ability to *link* equipment transfers to outcomes (such as measures of officer safety, crime rates, or police use of force) and other police activities (such as use and employment of transferred equipment and the extent to which transfers permit chronic underfunding of law enforcement functions). At a minimum, the transfer of responsibility for controlled equipment would seem to shift the focus to understanding the impact of the transfers on *policing and law enforcement* and away from the now well-documented operational components.

Fifth, and most importantly, moving accountability for controlled equipment to DoJ might help alleviate the issues of perception, if not also the reality, of police militarization. Such a move would seem likely to address the issue of police militarization by placing responsibility in an organization that has a more holistic view of law enforcement and more regular interaction with LEAs. On the other hand, this move could raise concerns that DoJ does not have sufficient expertise with some of the controlled equipment, such as armored personnel carriers, that it would now be overseeing. It seems likely that the PWG or another comparable interagency oversight body would offer an appropriate forum for resolving such dilemmas. At a minimum, such a transfer of responsibility would seem to offer a more coherent, focused bureaucratic structure in which to debate these issues by placing them squarely under the purview of an institution with the credibility, institutional knowledge, and expertise to make the necessary judgments about appropriate law enforcement use of transferred materiel.

Executive Order 13688

Federal Register / Vol. 80, No. 14 / Thursday, January 22, 2015 / Presidential Documents 3451

Presidential Documents

Executive Order 13688 of January 16, 2015

Federal Support for Local Law Enforcement Equipment Acquisition

By the authority vested in me as President by the Constitution and the laws of the United States of America, and in order to better coordinate Federal support for the acquisition of certain Federal equipment by State, local, and tribal law enforcement agencies, I hereby order as follows:

Section 1. *Policy.* For decades, the Federal Government has provided equipment to State, local, and tribal law enforcement agencies (LEAs) through excess equipment transfers (including GSA donations), asset forfeiture programs, and Federal grants. These programs have assisted LEAs as they carry out their critical missions to keep the American people safe. The equipment acquired by LEAs through these programs includes administrative equipment, such as office furniture and computers. But it also includes military and military-styled equipment, firearms, and tactical vehicles provided by the Federal Government, including property covered under 22 CFR part 121 and 15 CFR part 774 (collectively, "controlled equipment").

The Federal Government must ensure that careful attention is paid to standardizing procedures governing its provision of controlled equipment and funds for controlled equipment to LEAs. Moreover, more must be done to ensure that LEAs have proper training regarding the appropriate use of controlled equipment, including training on the protection of civil rights and civil liberties, and are aware of their obligations under Federal non-discrimination laws when accepting such equipment. To this end, executive departments and agencies (agencies) must better coordinate their efforts to operate and oversee these programs.

Sec. 2. *Law Enforcement Equipment Working Group.* (a) There is established an interagency Law Enforcement Equipment Working Group (Working Group) to identify agency actions that can improve Federal support for the acquisition of controlled equipment by LEAs, including by providing LEAs with controlled equipment that is appropriate to the needs of their community; ensuring that LEAs are properly trained to employ the controlled equipment they acquire; ensuring that LEAs adopt organizational and operational practices and standards that prevent the misuse or abuse of controlled equipment; and ensuring LEA compliance with civil rights requirements resulting from receipt of Federal financial assistance. The Working Group shall be co-chaired by the Secretary of Defense, Attorney General, and Secretary of Homeland Security. In addition to the Co-Chairs, the Working Group shall consist of the following members:

(i) the Secretary of the Treasury;

(ii) the Secretary of the Interior;

(iii) the Secretary of Education;

(iv) the Administrator of General Services;

(v) the Director of the Domestic Policy Council;

(vi) the Director of the Office of National Drug Control Policy;

(vii) the Director of the Office of Management and Budget;

(viii) the Assistant to the President for Intergovernmental Affairs and Public Engagement;

(ix) the Assistant to the President for Homeland Security and Counterterrorism;

(x) the Assistant to the President and Chief of Staff of the Office of the Vice President; and

(xi) the heads of such other agencies and offices as the Co-Chairs may, from time to time, designate.

(b) A member of the Working Group may designate a senior-level official who is from the member's agency or office and is a full-time officer or employee of the Federal Government to perform the day-to-day Working Group functions of the member. At the direction of the Co-Chairs, the Working Group may establish subgroups consisting exclusively of Working Group members or their designees under this subsection, as appropriate.

(c) There shall be an Executive Director of the Working Group, to be appointed by the Attorney General. The Executive Director shall determine the Working Group's agenda, convene regular meetings, and supervise its work under the direction of the Co-Chairs. The Department of Justice shall provide funding and administrative support for the Working Group to the extent permitted by law and within existing appropriations. Each agency shall bear its own expenses for participating in the Working Group.

Sec. 3. *Mission and Function of the Working Group.* (a) The Working Group shall provide specific recommendations to the President regarding actions that can be taken to improve the provision of Federal support for the acquisition of controlled equipment by LEAs, which may include, to the extent permitted by law:

(i) developing a consistent, Government-wide list of controlled equipment allowable for acquisition by LEAs, as well as a list of those items that can only be transferred with special authorization and use limitations;

(ii) establishing a process to review and approve proposed additions or deletions to the list of controlled equipment developed pursuant to paragraph (i) of this subsection;

(iii) harmonizing Federal programs so that they have consistent and transparent policies with respect to the acquisition of controlled equipment by LEAs;

(iv) requiring after-action analysis reports for significant incidents involving federally provided or federally funded controlled equipment;

(v) developing policies to ensure that LEAs abide by any limitations or affirmative obligations imposed on the acquisition of controlled equipment or receipt of funds to purchase controlled equipment from the Federal Government and the obligations resulting from receipt of Federal financial assistance;

(vi) planning the creation of a database that includes information about controlled equipment purchased or acquired through Federal programs;

(vii) ensuring a process for returning specified controlled equipment that was acquired from the Federal Government when no longer needed by an LEA;

(viii) requiring local civilian government (non-police) review of and authorization for LEAs' request for or acquisition of controlled equipment;

(ix) requiring that LEAs participating in Federal controlled equipment programs receive necessary training regarding appropriate use of controlled equipment and the implementation of obligations resulting from receipt of Federal financial assistance, including training on the protection of civil rights and civil liberties;

(x) providing uniform standards for suspending LEAs from Federal controlled equipment programs for specified violations of law, including civil rights laws, and ensuring those standards are implemented consistently across agencies; and

(xi) creating a process to monitor the sale or transfer of controlled equipment from the Federal Government or controlled equipment purchased with funds from the Federal Government by LEAs to third parties.

(b) The Working Group shall engage with external stakeholders, including appropriate State officials, law enforcement organizations, civil rights and civil liberties organizations, and academics, in developing the recommendations required by subsection (a) of this section.

(c) The Working Group shall provide the President with an implementation plan for each of its recommendations, which shall include concrete milestones with specific timetables and outcomes to be achieved.

Sec. 4. *Report.* Within 60 days of the date of this order, the Working Group shall provide the President with any recommendations and implementation plans it may have regarding the actions set forth in section 3(a)(i) and (ii) of this order. Within 120 days of the date of this order, the Working Group shall provide the President with any additional recommendations and implementation plans as set forth in section 3 of this order.

Sec. 5. *General Provisions.* (a) Nothing in this order shall be construed to impair or otherwise affect:

(i) the authority granted by law or Executive Order to an agency, or the head thereof; or

(ii) the functions of the Director of the Office of Management and Budget relating to budgetary, administrative, or legislative proposals.

(b) This order shall be implemented consistent with applicable law and subject to the availability of appropriations.

(c) This order is not intended to, and does not, create any right or benefit, substantive or procedural, enforceable at law or in equity by any party against the United States, its departments, agencies, or entities, its officers, employees, or agents, or any other person.

THE WHITE HOUSE,
January 16, 2015.

[FR Doc. 2015–01255
Filed 1–21–15; 11:15 am]
Billing code 3295–F5

APPENDIX B

Executive Order 13809

Federal Register
Vol. 82, No. 168
Thursday, August 31, 2017

Presidential Documents

Title 3—

The President

Executive Order 13809 of August 28, 2017

Restoring State, Tribal, and Local Law Enforcement's Access to Life-Saving Equipment and Resources

By the authority vested in me as President by the Constitution and the laws of the United States of America, it is hereby ordered as follows:

Section 1. *Revocation of Executive Order 13688.* Executive Order 13688 of January 16, 2015 (Federal Support for Local Law Enforcement Equipment Acquisition), is hereby revoked.

Sec. 2. *Revocation of Recommendations Issued Pursuant to Executive Order 13688.* The recommendations issued pursuant to Executive Order 13688 do not reflect the policy of the executive branch. All executive departments and agencies are directed, as of the date of this order and consistent with Federal law, to cease implementing those recommendations and, if necessary, to take prompt action to rescind any rules, regulations, guidelines, or policies implementing them.

Sec. 3. *General Provisions.* (a) Nothing in this order shall be construed to impair or otherwise affect:

(i) the authority granted by law to an executive department, agency, or the head thereof; or

(ii) the functions of the Director of the Office of Management and Budget relating to budgetary, administrative, or legislative proposals.

(b) This order shall be implemented consistent with applicable law and subject to the availability of appropriations.

(c) This order is not intended to, and does not, create any right or benefit, substantive or procedural, enforceable at law or in equity by any party against the United States, its departments, agencies, or entities, its officers, employees, or agents, or any other person.

THE WHITE HOUSE,
August 28, 2017.

[FR Doc. 2017–18679
Filed 8–30–17; 11:15 am]
Billing code 3295–F7–P

APPENDIX C

Standardized Interview Protocol for State Coordinators and State POCs

**Questions for STATE COORDINATORS for RAND Study,
"Evaluation of the Department of Defense's Excess Property Program:
Law Enforcement Agency Equipment Acquisition Policies, Guidance, and Outcomes"
Sponsored by DLA, J-3**

In response to a stipulation in the 2017 National Defense Authorization Act, the Defense Logistics Agency (DLA) J-3 has asked the RAND Corporation to conduct an evaluation of the Department of Defense's (DoD) Excess Property Program. To gather this information, we are interviewing law enforcement agencies, state coordinators, and other stakeholders about the program. This project is a follow-on to a similar effort conducted last year, and it is possible you or a member of your organization spoke to the project team during that effort.

The purpose of this discussion is to help us understand the program. Mr. Carlos Torres and his colleagues at the Law Enforcement Support Office (LESO) in Battle Creek, Michigan are available if you have any additional questions about this evaluation.

This discussion will last no more than one hour. The information you provide will be kept strictly confidential and used for research purposes only. Your responses will be combined with the responses of other interviewees to inform our research findings. The finished research products will not identify you in any way. Your participation will enable us to gain accurate and insightful knowledge about the program so that we can make informed recommendations to Congress.

Do you have any questions before we begin?

BACKGROUND

I'd like to start by learning some more about you and your agency.

- Please describe your position and responsibilities.
  - How long have you been in this position?
- How many LEAs in your state participate in the LESO Program?
- Do you have anybody helping you with the work?

Now, I'd like to talk about your state's experience with the LESO program.

- How long has (STATE) participated in the LESO program?
- What types of equipment have LEAs in your state obtained?

Next we would like to discuss how LESO equipment is currently categorized. As you may know, LESO equipment falls under 2 general categories: controlled and uncontrolled equipment. While the title of uncontrolled equipment is passed to LEAs after one year, DOD retains ownership of controlled items into perpetuity.

Controlled items are often military-specific items—such as night-vision goggles, robots, communication equipment, and binoculars. This type of military equipment is DOD-controlled. Executive Order, or EO–controlled items are a subset of DOD-controlled items. These items include aircraft, armored vehicles, weapons, and crowd control equipment. Acquiring EO-controlled items requires community-approval of justifications, adoption of General Policing Standards and Specific Controlled Equipment Standards, collection of certain information, and additional controls on the transfer of the equipment.

- Are the current categorizations of LESO equipment, that is, uncontrolled, DOD or EO controlled, prohibited, appropriate? For example, is there equipment included in any category which should be in another category instead?
- What has changed in the program as a result of the Executive Order?
- What differences, if any, are there in the LESO process between acquiring EO-controlled versus DOD-controlled equipment?
- LESO prioritizes distribution of some controlled equipment for use in counter-drug, counter terror, or border security operations. Do organizations in your state use any of the controlled equipment it has received for any of these purposes? Please explain.
- Have you recommended law enforcement agencies include the keywords "counterdrug," "counter terror," or "border security operations" in their justifications for requesting this equipment? In your experience, how does LESO use these

keywords to prioritize distribution? Are there aspects that could be changed or improved?

- Some LEAs may have previously received equipment that was later recategorized as "prohibited" under the EO, was recalled by LESO, and can no longer be provided through the LESO program. Did your state have any such items?
  - Has the EO designation of "prohibited" changed whether departments in your state have this type of equipment in their inventory? For example, did they get this equipment from another source? Where?
- Are there scenarios where utilizing controlled property adds risk to officers and/or citizens?

AGENCY INVENTORY

- If it had not been available through the LESO program, would departments in your state have obtained *uncontrolled* equipment it received from the LESO Program through another source? How (e.g., bought, other federal grants, donations)?
- If it had not been available through the LESO program, would departments in your state have obtained *controlled* equipment it received from the LESO Program through another source? How (e.g., bought, other federal grants, donations)?
- How much does it cost your state to participate in the LESO program?
- Do you check to see if LEAs already have similar equipment in their inventory before approving the request? Do you ask why they want more of the equipment?
- Do you ensure LEAs use this equipment for law enforcement purposes? Do you make decisions about the appropriateness of an LEA obtaining this equipment?
- How do you prioritize LEA requests? Are there any common themes for why you deny requests?

Ownership of uncontrolled equipment transfers from LESO to the law enforcement agency after one year. Some police departments then sell the equipment.

- Do agencies in your state sell any of the equipment received from the LESO program? If so, which items, why did they sell them, and who did they sell them to?

SUSPENSIONS

- Has your state ever been suspended from the LESO program? If so, why were you suspended?
  - When and how long? Did you agree with the suspension?
  - What, if any, internal changes did your state make as a result?

  - How did your interactions with the LESO Program change as a result?
  - What changes could LESO make to help prevent departments or states from being suspended?

LAW ENFORCEMENT MISSION

- How does the controlled equipment agencies in your state have received through the LESO Program help agencies with its law enforcement mission? How does the uncontrolled equipment help your state's agencies with their law enforcement mission?
  - PROBE: officer safety, natural disaster preparation, crime reduction/prevention efforts?

Nationally, there has been an increase in perceived tensions between law enforcement and the public, and some believe this a result of a perceived increase in the "militarization" of law enforcement.

- How do you consider public perceptions when making decisions about whether to approve requested controlled equipment?
- How do agencies in your state address the requirement to obtain consent from the highest elected official for requests for controlled equipment?
- Has your state's position on whether to obtain or how it uses certain types of equipment changed over the past few years as a result of changing public perceptions? How?
- How does your state's agencies determine whether they need controlled equipment?
- In your experience, what role do the state coordinator and LESO play in determining whether law enforcement agencies should be allowed to obtain a piece of controlled equipment?
  - Should this be changed?
  - Could it be improved?
  - Is there an appropriate level of oversight by LESO and the state coordinator, too much, too little, or should another entity, such as the Department of Justice (DOJ), be involved?

APPENDIX D

Standardized Interview Protocol for LEA Officials

Questions for LAW ENFORCEMENT AGENCIES for RAND Study, "Evaluation of the Department of Defense's Excess Property Program: Law Enforcement Agency Equipment Acquisition Policies, Guidance, and Outcomes"
Sponsored by DLA, J-3

In response to a Congressional mandate in the 2017 National Defense Authorization Act, the Defense Logistics Agency (DLA) J-3 has asked the RAND Corporation to conduct an evaluation of the Department of Defense's (DoD) Excess Property Program. To gather this information, we are interviewing Law Enforcement Agencies (LEAs), state coordinators, and other stakeholders about the program. This project is a follow-on to a similar effort conducted last year, and it is possible you or a member of your organization spoke to the project team during that effort. The purpose of this discussion is to help us understand all aspects of the program from the perspective of the LEAs that receive the excess property. If you have any questions about our evaluation, Mr. Carlos Torres, Chief, DLA Disposition Services Law Enforcement Support Office and his colleagues at the Battle Creek, MI office are available.

This discussion will last no more than one hour. The information you provide will be kept strictly confidential and used for research purposes only. Your identity will not be revealed to your State Coordinator or the DLA LESO. Your responses will be combined with the responses of other interviewees to inform our research findings.

Do you have any questions before we begin?

BACKGROUND

I'd like to start by learning some more about you and your agency.

- Please describe your position and responsibilities.

- How long have you been in this position?
- How many full-time sworn personnel work for your agency?
- How many hours a week does your staff dedicate to this program?

Now I'd like to talk about your agency's experience with the LESO program.

- How long has the (AGENCY NAME) participated in the LESO program?
- What types of equipment have you obtained? (PROBE AS NEEDED TO IDENTIFY CONTROLLED AND UNCONTROLLED PROPERTY)

- Are the current categorizations of LESO equipment appropriate? For example, is there equipment included in any category which should be in another category instead?

- LESO prioritizes distribution of some controlled equipment for use in counter-drug, counter terror, or border security operations. Does your organization use any of the controlled equipment it has received for any of these purposes? Please explain.

- Did your organization include the keywords "counterdrug," "counter terror," or "border security operations" in your justification for requesting this equipment? In your experience, how does LESO use these keywords to prioritize distribution? Are there aspects that could be changed or improved?

- Some LEAs may have previously received equipment that was later recategorized as "prohibited" under the EO, was recalled by LESO, and can no longer be provided through the LESO program. Did your department have any such items?
  - Has the designation of "prohibited" changed whether your department has this type of equipment in your inventory? For example, did you get this equipment from another source? Where?
- Has the designation of "controlled" changed whether your department has this type of equipment in your inventory?
  - If so, did you get this equipment from another source? Why did you look for this equipment elsewhere?

AGENCY INVENTORY

- If it had not been available through the LESO program, would your department have obtained *uncontrolled* equipment it has received through the LESO Program through another source? How (e.g., bought, other federal grants, donations)?
- If it had not been available through the LESO program, would your department have obtained *controlled* equipment it has received through the LESO Program through another source? How (e.g. bought, other federal grants, donations)?
- What would the impact be on your department's budget if the LESO program did not exist?
  - If the LESO program did not exist, in general, what percentage of the controlled equipment that you received through the LESO Program would you have bought with your department's own budget? What percentage would you have obtained using other grants, and what percentage would you have not obtained? What about for uncontrolled equipment?
  - If you had to estimate, how much do you think your department has saved (i.e. counting only equipment you would have obtained using other resources) by participating in the LESO program?
    - How has your department used the funds it has saved by participating in the LESO program?
  - How much does it cost your department to participate in the LESO program?

- What would the impact be on your agency of not obtaining the controlled equipment you would not have received without the LESO program? The uncontrolled equipment?

Ownership of uncontrolled equipment transfers from LESO to the law enforcement agency after one year. Some police departments then sell the equipment.

- Has your agency sold any of the equipment it received from the LESO program? If so, which items, why did you sell them, who did you sell them to, and how much did you receive for them?

SUSPENSIONS

- Has your department ever been suspended from the LESO program? If so, why were you suspended?
  - When and how long? Did you agree with the suspension?
  - What, if any, internal changes did your department make as a result?

- How did your interactions with your state coordinator or the LESO Program change as a result?
- What changes could LESO make to help prevent departments from being suspended?

LAW ENFORCEMENT MISSION

- How does the controlled equipment you have received through the LESO Program help your department with its law enforcement mission? How does the uncontrolled equipment help your department with its law enforcement mission?
  - PROBE: officer safety, natural disaster preparation, crime reduction/prevention efforts?

Nationally, there has been an increase in perceived tensions between law enforcement and the public, and some believe this a result of a perceived increase in the "militarization" of law enforcement.

- How does your department consider public perceptions when making decisions about whether to request controlled equipment?
- How does your department address the requirement to obtain consent from the highest elected official for requests for controlled equipment?
- Has your department's position on whether to obtain or how it uses certain types of equipment changed over the past few years as a result of changing public perceptions? How?
- How does your department determine whether it needs controlled equipment?
- In your experience, what role do the state coordinator and LESO play in determining whether your department should be allowed to obtain a piece of controlled equipment?
  - Should this be changed?
  - Could it be improved?
  - Is there an appropriate level of oversight by LESO and the state coordinator, too much, too little, or should another entity, such as the Department of Justice (DOJ), be involved?
- Other than what we have already discussed, what are the practical downsides to obtaining LESO equipment? For example, administrative, training, or operational issues?
  - What is the cost of maintaining the program for your department?

References

ACLU—*See* American Civil Liberties Union.

American Civil Liberties Union, *War Comes Home: The Excessive Militarization of American Policing*, June 2014a. As of August 4, 2017:
https://www.aclu.org/report/war-comes-home-excessive-militarization-american-police

———, "Coalition Including ACLU Asks Defense Secretary for Moratorium on 1033 Program that Militarizes Local Police," press release, October 27, 2014b. As of August 4, 2017:
https://www.aclu.org/other/coalition-including-aclu-asks-defense-secretary-moratorium-1033-program-militarizes-local

———, "Statement on Freddie Gray and Police/Community Conflict in Baltimore," press release, April 28, 2015. As of July 3, 2017:
https://www.aclu.org/news/statement-freddie-gray-and-policecommunity-conflict-baltimore

"Are Federal Programs that Provide Military Equipment to State and Local Police Departments Effective?" *Congressional Digest*, Vol. 94, No. 2, February 2015. As of August 4, 2017:
http://congressionaldigest.com/issue/law-enforcement-and-community-relations/#gsc.tab=0

Balko, Radley, "Pentagon Suspends Program That Gives Military Weapons to Cops," *Huffington Post*, June 11, 2012. As of June 28, 2017:
http://www.huffingtonpost.com/2012/06/11/pentagon-suspends-weapons-program-cops-military_n_1585328.html

Bauman, Dan, "On Campus, Grenade Launchers, M-16s, and Armored Vehicles," *Chronicle of Higher Education,* September 11, 2014. As of August 4, 2017:
http://www.chronicle.com/article/On-Campus-Grenade-Launchers/148749/

Bove, Vincenzo, and Evelina Gavrilova, "Police Officer on the Frontline or a Soldier? The Effect of Police Militarization on Crime," *American Economic Journal: Economic Policy*, Vol. 9, No. 3, 2017, pp. 1–18.

DDS—*See* Defense Logistics Agency Disposition Services.

Defense Logistics Agency, "Defense Logistics Agency Instruction DLAI 4140.11," December 22, 2016.

———, "Executive Order 13809 Implementation Plan," October 2017.

———, presentation to RAND by Michael Johnson, DLA J349, October 27, 2017.

Defense Logistics Agency Disposition Services, "Controlled Property Definition," fact sheet, April 18, 2017.

DoD—*See* U.S. Department of Defense.

DODM—*See* U.S. Department of Defense Manual.

DoJ—*See* U.S. Department of Justice.

Else, Daniel H., "The '1033 Program,' Department of Defense Support to Law Enforcement," Congressional Research Service, August 28, 2014.

Executive Office of the President, "Review: Federal Support for Local Law Enforcement Equipment Acquisition," Washington, D.C., December 2014. As of August 4, 2017:
https://obamawhitehouse.archives.gov/sites/default/files/docs/federal_support_for_local_law_enforcement_equipment_acquisition.pdf

———, Executive Order 13809, "Restoring State, Tribal, and Local Law Enforcement's Access to Lifesaving Equipment and Resources," August 28, 2017.

Fraternal Order of Police, "The Trump Administration: The First 100 Days," undated. As of August 4, 2017:
https://fop.net/CmsDocument/Doc/TrumpFirst100Days.pdf

"Freddie Gray's Death in Police Custody—What We Know," BBC News, May 23, 2016. As of July 3, 2017:
http://www.bbc.com/news/world-us-canada-32400497

GAO—*See* U.S. General Accounting Office, U.S. Government Accountability Office.

Gould-Wartofsky, Michael, "The Wars Come Home," *Huffington Post*, May 5, 2015. As of July 3, 2017:
http://www.huffingtonpost.com/michael-gouldwartofsky/the-wars-come-home_b_7213830.html

Harris, Matthew C., Jinseong Park, Donald J. Bruce, and Matthew N. Murray, "Peacekeeping Force: Effects of Providing Tactical Equipment to Local Law Enforcement," *American Economic Journal: Economic Policy*, Vol. 3, No. 3, 2017, pp. 291–313.

H.R.—*See* U.S. House Resolution.

Institute for Intergovernmental Research, *After-Action Assessment of the Police Response to the August 2014 Demonstrations in Ferguson, Missouri*, Community Oriented Policing Services, September 3, 2015. As of August 4, 2017:
https://ric-zai-inc.com/ric.php?page=detail&id=COPS-P317

Johnson, Michael, "DLA EO 13809 Implementation Plan, Revocation of EO 13688," federal brief, Defense Logistics Agency, J349, June 5, 2017.

Law Enforcement Equipment Working Group, *Recommendations Pursuant to the Executive Order 13688, Federal Support for Local Law Enforcement Equipment Acquisition,* May 2015. As of March 16, 2018:
https://www.hsdl.org/?abstract&did=765878

———, "Enhanced Criteria for Institutions of Higher Education (IHE) Applicants," February 2016. As of August 4, 2017:
https://www.bja.gov/publications/EnhancedCriteriaforInstitutionsofHigherEducationApplicants.pdf

Li, Shirley, "The Evolution of Police Militarization in Ferguson and Beyond," *The Atlantic,* August 15, 2014. As of June 28, 2017:
https://www.theatlantic.com/national/archive/2014/08/the-evolution-of-police-militarization-in-ferguson-and-beyond/376107/

Miller, Zeke J., "Obama Voices Concerns on Police Militarization in Wake of Ferguson," *Time,* August 18, 2014. As of June 28, 2017:
http://time.com/3138267/obama-ferguson-police-militarization/

Office of the Inspector General, *Logistics: Law Enforcement Support Office Excess Property Program (D-2003-101)*, U.S. Department of Defense, Washington, D.C., June 13, 2003.

Pollard, Michael, and Matthew D. Baird, *The RAND American Life Panel: Technical Description*, Santa Monica, Calif.: RAND Corporation, RR-1651, 2017. As of November 22, 2017: https://www.rand.org/pubs/research_reports/RR1651.html

Principal Deputy Under Secretary of Defense, Acquisition, Technology, and Logistics, "Oversight of Federal Programs for Equipping State and Local Law Enforcement," letter to U.S. Senator Claire McCaskill, January 19, 2017.

PWG—*See* Law Enforcement Equipment Working Group.

Reaves, Brian A., *Local Police Departments 2013: Personnel, Policies, and Practices*, NCJ 248677, Washington, D.C.: U.S. Department of Justice, Office of Justice Programs, Bureau of Justice Statistics, May 2015.

Ridgeway, Greg, Terry L. Schell, Brian Gifford, Jessica Saunders, Susan Turner, Kevin Jack Riley, and Travis L. Dixon, *Police-Community Relations in Cincinnati*, Santa Monica, Calif.: RAND Corporation, MG-853-CC, 2009. As of March 14, 2018: https://www.rand.org/pubs/monographs/MG853.html

Selyukh, Alina, "Bomb Robots: What Makes Killing in Dallas Different and What Happens Next?" NPR, July 8, 2016. As of July 3, 2017: http://www.npr.org/sections/thetwo-way/2016/07/08/485262777/for-the-first-time-police-used-a-bomb-robot-to-kill

Shinkman, Paul D., "Ferguson and the Militarization of Police," *U.S. News*, August 14, 2014. As of June 28, 2017: https://www.usnews.com/news/articles/2014/08/14/ferguson-and-the-shocking-nature-of-us-police-militarization

Sklansky, David Alan, "Police and Democracy," *Michigan Law Review*, Vol. 103, No. 7, June 2005, pp. 1699–1830.

Szoldra, Paul, "This Is the Terrifying Result of the Militarization of Police," *Business Insider*, August 12, 2014. As of June 28, 2017: http://www.businessinsider.com/police-militarization-ferguson-2014-8

Taft, Isabelle, "Police Use of Robot to Kill Dallas Suspect Unprecedented, Experts Say," *Texas Tribune*, July 8, 2016. As of July 3, 2017: https://www.texastribune.org/2016/07/08/use-robot-kill-dallas-suspect-first-experts-say/

Torres, Carlos, "Law Enforcement Support Office (LESO) Program," Federal Law Enforcement Agencies brief, Defense Logistics Agency Disposition Services, June 5, 2017.

U.S. Code, Title 10, Section 380, Enhancement of Cooperation with Civilian Law Enforcement Officials.

U.S. Code, Title 10, Section 2576a, Excess Personal Property: Sale or Donation for Law Enforcement Activities.

U.S. Department of Defense Manual 4160.21-M, *Defense Materiel Disposition Manual*, Office of the Deputy Under Secretary of Defense (Logistics), Washington, D.C., August 1997.

U.S. Department of Defense Manual 4160.28-V2, *Defense Demilitarization: Demilitarization Coding*, June 7, 2011.

U.S. Department of Defense Manual 4160.21, *Defense Materiel Disposition Manual: Instructions for Hazardous Property and Other Special Processing Materiel*, Vol. 1–4, October 22, 2015.

U.S. Department of Justice, "Conduct of Law Enforcement Agencies," webpage, updated September 14, 2017. As of May 3, 2018:
https://www.justice.gov/crt/conduct-law-enforcement-agencies

U.S. Department of Justice Office of Justice Programs, Bureau of Justice Statistics, *Law Enforcement Management and Administrative Statistics (LEMAS) Survey, 1987–2013*, NCJ-248677, May 2015.

U.S. General Accounting Office, *Inventory Management: Better Controls Needed to Prevent Misuse of Excess DOD Property*, OSI/NSIAD-00-147, April 28, 2000. As of August 4, 2017:
http://www.gao.gov/products/OSI/NSIAD-00-147

———, "Defense Inventory: Control Weaknesses Leave Restricted and Hazardous Excess Property Vulnerable to Improper Use, Loss, and Theft," GAO-02-75, January 25, 2002. As of August 4, 2017:
http://www.gao.gov/products/GAO-02-75

U.S. Government Accountability Office, *DOD Excess Property: Management Control Breakdowns Result in Substantial Waste and Inefficiency*, GAO-05-277, Washington, D.C., June 7, 2005. As of August 4, 2017:
http://www.gao.gov/products/GAO-05-277

———, *Control Breakdowns Present Significant Security Risk and Continuing Waste and Inefficiency*, GAO-06-943, Washington, D.C., July 25, 2006. As of August 4, 2017:
http://www.gao.gov/products/GAO-06-981T

———, *Actions Needed to Improve the Defense Logistics Agency's Inventory Management*, GAO-14-495, Washington, D.C., June 19, 2014. As of August 4, 2017:
http://www.gao.gov/products/GAO-14-495

———, *Excess Personal Property: DOD Should Further Reassess the Priorities of Its Disposal Process*, GAO-16-44, January 29, 2016. As of August 4, 2017:
https://www.gao.gov/products/GAO-16-44

———, *DOD Excess Property: Enhanced Controls Needed for Access to Excess Controlled Property*, GAO-17-532, July 18, 2017. As of August 4, 2017:
http://www.gao.gov/products/GAO-17-532

U.S. House of Representatives Committee Repository, "Hearing: The Department of Defense Excess Property Program in Support of U.S. Law Enforcement Agencies: An Overview of DOD Authorities, Roles, Responsibilities, and Implementation of Section 1033 of the 1997 National Defense Authorization Act," agenda, Washington, D.C., Subcommittee on Oversight and Investigations (Committee on Armed Services), November 13, 2014. As of July 3, 2017:
http://docs.house.gov/Committee/Calendar/ByEvent.aspx?EventID=102730

U.S. House Resolution 5478, Stop Militarizing Law Enforcement Act, 113th Congress, September 16, 2014.

U.S. House Resolution 426, Protecting Lives Using Surplus Equipment Act of 2017, 115th Congress, January 10, 2017.

U.S. Senate Committee on Homeland Security and Governmental Affairs, "Oversight of Federal Programs for Equipping State and Local Law Enforcement," hearing transcript, September 9, 2014. As of June 28, 2017:
https://www.hsgac.senate.gov/hearings/oversight-of-federal-programs-for-equipping-state-and-local-law-enforcement

Vincent, James, "Everything We Know About the Bomb Robot Used by Dallas Police," *The Verge*, July 8, 2016. As of July 3, 2017:
https://www.theverge.com/2016/7/8/12129348/dallas-shooting-bomb-robot

Wagner, Dennis, "Pinal Sheriff's Office Stockpiles, Prepares to Sell Military Equipment," *Arizona Republic*, May 19, 2012. As of June 28, 2017:
http://archive.azcentral.com/news/politics/20120504pinal-county-surplus-military-equipment.html

White House Office of the Press Secretary, "Press Briefing by Press Secretary Josh Earnest, 8/25/2014," August 25, 2014. As of June 28, 2017:
https://obamawhitehouse.archives.gov/the-press-office/2014/08/25/press-briefing-press-secretary-josh-earnest-8252014

———, "Executive Order—Federal Support for Local Law Enforcement Equipment Acquisition," Executive Order 13688, President Barack Obama, Washington, D.C., January 16, 2015.